The Fantasy of Individuality

Almudena Hernando

The Fantasy of Individuality

On The Sociohistorical Construction
Of the Modern Subject

Copernicus Books is a brand of Springer

Almudena Hernando
Departamento de Prehistoria
Universidad Complutense Madrid
Madrid, Spain

Copyrights:
Spanish Edition: *La fantasia de la individualidad. Sobre la construcción sociohistórica del sujeto moderno*. Katz Editores, Buenos Aires/Madrid.

Copyright for the translation: Pedro Fermin Maguire

ISBN 978-3-319-60719-1   ISBN 978-3-319-60720-7 (eBook)
DOI 10.1007/978-3-319-60720-7

Library of Congress Control Number: 2017942805

© Springer International Publishing AG 2017
1st edition: © Katz Editores 2012
This work is subject to copyright. All rights are reserved by the Publisher, whether the whole or part of the material is concerned, specifically the rights of translation, reprinting, reuse of illustrations, recitation, broadcasting, reproduction on microfilms or in any other physical way, and transmission or information storage and retrieval, electronic adaptation, computer software, or by similar or dissimilar methodology now known or hereafter developed.
The use of general descriptive names, registered names, trademarks, service marks, etc. in this publication does not imply, even in the absence of a specific statement, that such names are exempt from the relevant protective laws and regulations and therefore free for general use.
The publisher, the authors and the editors are safe to assume that the advice and information in this book are believed to be true and accurate at the date of publication. Neither the publisher nor the authors or the editors give a warranty, express or implied, with respect to the material contained herein or for any errors or omissions that may have been made. The publisher remains neutral with regard to jurisdictional claims in published maps and institutional affiliations.

Printed on acid-free paper

This Copernicus imprint is published by Springer Nature
The registered company is Springer International Publishing AG
The registered company address is: Gewerbestrasse 11, 6330 Cham, Switzerland

*To my colleagues at the Prehistory Department.
of the Complutense University of Madrid.
With gratitude.*

Acknowledgments

This book is the result of many years of work, questioning, and growth, both intellectual and personal. The data discussed here were obtained on several research stays at the Universities of California (Los Angeles and Berkeley), Chicago and Harvard. Each one of these stays lasted for at least 3 months and took place between 1995 and 2004. They were made possible by three research scholarships (two *Becas Complutense del Amo* and one Harvard *Real Colegio Complutense Grant*) and a mobility license from the Spanish Ministry of Education and Science. After very intense and concentrated work, I produced an initial draft back in Harvard between the months of March and May of 2011, this time thanks to a new scholarship from the Real Colegio Complutense and funding from the Spanish Ministry of Science and Innovation (project HAR2009-08666). I would like to thank the Department of Social Anthropology, particularly Professor Bar-Yosef and Director Gary Urton, for hosting me as a visiting scholar. But I am especially grateful to the director of the RCC, Ángel Sáenz Badillos, for the atmosphere of work and respect, for the kindness and support and the stimulus and freedom I was met with at the *Colegio*, as well as for running this institution in a way which facilitated convivial encounters, both intellectual and personal. I am indebted to Elizabeth Kline and Cristina Herrero for their care and support at a time when I suffered an accident and had to wrestle with the peculiar functioning of the US health system.

In an academic world where the natural and social sciences are becoming so equated that it is harder and harder to choose research topics, I have the fortune of belonging to a generation which could choose research topics irrespective of net result productivity. In fact, beyond a certain point in my career, I have even had the feeling that my choices about research phases, or the direction of the next project, my next book, etc., were no more dictated by myself than by the very logic of my arguments and reasoning. My impression was that certain issues demanded attention with a weight and urgency which I could not but attend. Research itself dictated my path and not vice versa.

My steps along this path have taken me further and further away from the specialization which has traditionally characterized my disciplinary area, the study of prehistory. For this reason, I would like to express my most sincere gratitude to the

Department of Prehistory at the Complutense University of Madrid, which I have been part of for almost 30 years. I have enjoyed the immense fortune and privilege of working at a department where most pursue knowledge in their respective areas in an honest, intelligent, and generous manner, creating a personal and intellectual atmosphere which has almost no match in any academic context. The feeling of uttermost respect toward the changes in the direction of my research and the support and friendship I have found in some of its members have been essential in defining my own true intellectual and academic interests. Without this measure of freedom, it would have been impossible to follow the logic of a line of research which has grown more and more inseparable from my own life concerns. Therefore, I would like to dedicate this book to them in return, as, without their help, it would not have come into existence.

Along the winding road of my research path, I have undertaken a number of projects with contemporary indigenous groups, in an effort to understand the way in which the world is perceived, along with one's own place in it, from the point of view of those born into societies without writing, oral societies. My latest research project of this type has been with the Awá-Guajá group, which I refer to repeatedly in this text. The project was funded by the Ministry of Science and Innovation (research and development project HUM2006-06276) and entitled *Ethno-archaeology of the Awá-Guajá, a group of hunter-gatherers in transition toward agriculture (Maranhão-Brasil)*. The team included researchers Elizabeth Beserra Coelho, Gustavo Politis, and Alfredo González Ruibal. I am grateful to the Brazilian FUNAI and CNPq for the due authorizations and permissions and of course to the Awá for their patience, generosity, and hospitality.

As I embarked on my initial fieldwork with oral populations, my personal life unfolded too, and it eventually became clear to me that men and women approach the same problems from very different perspectives and, especially, that the solutions we find to them are radically different. I realized how men and women generally have different ways of construing their identities and that, in the same way as encounters between oral groups and modern societies invariably result in modern society retaining its power, in encounters between men and women, all too often men retain the mechanisms that will eventually hand power over to them. I began to wonder about the connections between both dynamics, between these two forms of subordination, and about the possible relationship that might exist between the identity of oral societies and female gender identity.

At the Institute of Feminist Research (*Instituto de Investigaciones Feministas*) of the Complutense University of Madrid, I have found a haven of intellectual discussion and emotional support from which to begin to reflect about women's issues and identities from a perspective still unknown to most prehistorians and archaeologists. And yet, I have also found colleagues in the field of archaeology who share these interests and have provided true companionship and the necessary stimulus to pursue them. Among these colleagues, I would like to mention Margarita Sánchez-Romero, and, very particularly, Sandra Montón. Sandra directed the research and development project HAR2009-08666, financed by the Spanish Ministry of Science and Innovation, among the results of which is this book that she so enthusiastically (conceptually and economically) supported so it could be put into print. In Sandra I have always found encouragement, stimulus, recognition, and companionship.

My multidisciplinary vision of knowledge has gradually required increased teamwork, which materialized into two discussion groups, guided by the sheer pursuit of knowledge and aimed at supporting the reflections of participants. The first of these was devoted to modern theories of cultural analysis. I would like to mention here Alfredo González Ruibal and Víctor Fernández, whose initiative and contributions of novel and exciting texts virtually spawned the group, as well as Núria Gallego, Manuel Sánchez-Elipe, Lucía Moragón, Beatriz Marín, Sandra Lozano, José Luis Hergueta, Alfonso Fraguas, and so many other participants who also contributed to those group discussions.

But it has been within the Group of Readings on Women and Culture, created in collaboration with (and by the initiative of) psychoanalyst and friend Nora Levinton, that I have found a space for friendly and intelligent reflection about some of the specific topics dealt with in this book. The permanent core of this group also includes Julia Herce, Maite San Miguel, Fátima Arranz, Carolina Meloni, and María Luisa Lasheras. Although we all share a critical feminist stance, each one of us comes from a different professional background and—in my opinion, for that very reason—contributes to the stimulus and growth of the group in their own way. The experience of this interaction has taught me that, while intellectual work has a necessarily individuated, personal, and nontransferable aspect, teamwork allows us to understand the limitations of our own thought, to come to terms with the hindrances of our own paradigms, and to discover new problems which are only visible from the fresh and uncontaminated look of an outsider to one's own specialized field. On the other hand, as I have always learned from the experience of teaching, emotional communication is fundamental for intellectual growth and builds the necessary bridges for the creative development of those on the receiving side of information flows. In this respect, I do not think that personal interaction can be substituted for that sustained through computers (or books). Direct and face-to-face emotional relationships create possibilities for a type of intellectual process which cannot quite be activated by machines or mediating artifacts. My experience is that thought is not only the result of increased information but of many psychological processes of an emotional kind (stimulus, recognition, valuing, legitimation, etc.) which have all taken place in these reading groups.

Intellectual and emotional alliances with other women sharing the same problems, questions, and confusions as have defined my own life so far have been essential to my understanding that these had nothing to do with any deficiencies or insufficiencies of mine but, rather, that they manifested a wider and more general problem, to which I have devoted this book. These alliances include a very specific group of friends, particularly Julia Herce, Nora Levinton, Pilar Aguilar, Fátima Arranz, Pilar Rubio, and Laura Freixas. Without them I could not possibly have found the self-confidence to make the arguments I have made here. And it is to them, along with Carolina Meloni, that I owe readings and relevant comments on parts of a first draft of this book.

To Juan Gutiérrez, Ángela Dewar, and Ana, Sofía, Sally, and Gabriela Gutiérrez-Dewar I owe the privilege of having found a second family, where intellectual recognition is as important as the unconditional love they profess for each other and toward those fortunate enough to be part of their *extended* core. The importance of emotions must have become clearer to me through them, thanks to their warm and generous capacity to express affection with the only limitations of scrupulous and delicate care and respect for others.

Finally, this book is the result of an entire life experience in a family of five sisters and one brother who stay very united and whose conflicts, silences, needs, and resolutions have provided the raw material of all my reflections.

My most sincere gratitude and most profound affection go to all of them.

Addenda to the English Version

It would be unfair to end these acknowledgments simply by translating those of the first Spanish version of the present book. This translation is the result of the collaboration of several people who I cannot but mention. Sandra Montón has once again proven herself unflinching in providing all the necessary support for this book to appear in its present English version. P. Fermín Maguire has turned out to be the best option to translate it, with his great patience, care, and keenness to adjust to the nuances I repeatedly asked him to check. I would also like to insist here (again) on my gratitude to Ángela Dewar for her firm friendship, her generosity, and her willingness to assist me in the many issues and requests that sprang from my many questionings. Finally, with the joy of being able to put into writing my gratitude for far longer than affects this translation, I would like to thank Antonio and Benedicte Gilman for their ever-generous friendship from the bottom of my heart. Antonio opened doors to facilitate my research stays at American universities, without which this book would never have come into being. And both have always granted me intelligent and loving support throughout the years and on both sides of the Atlantic Ocean. I am indebted to them for the exceedingly generous final proofreading of this text, which I, abusing our friendship, asked for and they, attesting to their profound human and professional qualities, acceded to.

Contents

1 **General Approach** 1
  1.1 1
  1.2 2
  1.3 6
  1.4 9
  1.5 10
  1.6 11
  1.7 12
  1.8 13
  References 15

2 **Sex and Gender** 19
  References 23

3 **The Origin** 25
  3.1 The Origin of Humanity and Primate Behavior Patterns 27
  3.2 What Do We Humans Have that Bonobos Lack? 34
  3.3 Recapitulation and Starting Point 36
  References 38

4 **Relational Identity (or Identity When One Has No Power over the World)** 41
  4.1 Relational Identity 41
  4.2 Gender in So-Called Egalitarian Societies 46
  References 54

5 **Individuality (or Identity When One Has Power over the World)** 57
  References 66

6	**Relational Identity/Individuated Identity:**	
	The Appearance of Things	69
	6.1 The Historical Construction of Identity	70
	References	77
7	**The Fantasy of Individuality I: Women and Gender Identity**	79
	7.1 The Repression of Women's Mobility and Writing	87
	References	93
8	**The Fantasy of Individuality II:**	
	Men's (Unconscious) Performance of Relational Identity	97
	References	105
9	***Dependent* Individuality and *Independent* Individuality**	107
	9.1 Dependent Individuality	107
	9.2 Independent Individuality	110
	References	117
10	**Sex and Gender All over Again**	119
	10.1 On Gender	119
	10.2 On Sexuality	121
	References	123
11	**Conclusion**	125
	11.1	125
	11.2	126
	11.3	129
	11.4	131
	11.5	133
	11.6	136
	References	137
Index		139

About the Author

Almudena Hernando is a professor at the Department of Prehistory and member of the Institute of Feminist Research at the Complutense University, Madrid. Her research focuses on the theoretical basis underlying identity construction, with special attention to oral societies, and to women in the Western world. She carried out fieldwork among the horticulturalists Q'eqchí (Guatemala) and the hunter-gatherers Awá (Amazonas, Brazil), and in this moment, she develops a research project among the hoe agriculturalists Gumuz and Dats'in from Ethiopia. She has been an invited researcher in the Universities of California (Los Angeles and Berkeley), Chicago and Harvard. She has written several books such as *Los Primeros Agricultores de la Península Ibérica* (Ed. Síntesis) and *Arqueología de la Identidad* (Akal), and she has coedited and participated in others such as *La Construcción de la Subjetividad Femenina* (Institute of Feminist Research, Madrid), *Desean las Mujeres El Poder? Cinco Reflexiones En Torno a Un Deseo Conflictivo* (Minerva), and *Mujeres, Hombres, Poder. Subjetividades en Conflicto* (Traficantes de Sueños).

Chapter 1
General Approach

1.1

I think I have never fully trusted appearances, maybe because my mother used to love dressing me and my twin sister in the exact same clothes—despite the fact that we were like chalk and cheese—and even our third and fourth sisters. And although even as adults we have always had an excellent relationship, beneath that delightful image of harmonious child synchronization lay as many conflicts as one might expect of the six siblings we eventually came to be.

This might also have been what, unbeknownst to me, made me want to study archaeology; after devoting an entire doctoral thesis to the Calcolithic period in the Spanish southeast, I realized that I was hardly interested at all in what had happened around 2500 BC. Whatever reason had driven me there became an utter mystery to me. And yet it is crystal clear to me now that without prehistory and archaeology, I could not possibly think about the things that interest me in the precise way I am interested in thinking about them. It took me quite some time to arrive at what Freud and Foucault had already understood a long time before me: what I found most attractive about archaeology was that, used metaphorically, it provided a long-term genealogical and analytical procedure, a method that teaches us to dig deeper into the roots and foundations of visible processes, bringing to our attention the more profound logic that renders them meaningful rather than the appearance that their expressions may adopt at any given time. I also came to understand that prehistory teaches us to consider origins as one of the essential keys of these processes, a fundamental parameter without which they cannot be fully understood. But above all, I grasped that the study of material culture, the disciplinary focus of archaeology, offers a particularly interesting tool for the study of society for those of us who do not want to be fooled by appearances, for it pays attention to what people actually do, and not, as is the case with history, to what they have decided to put into words about themselves.

Applying an archaeological gaze to present-day societies, whether indigenous or industrial, sheds light on very interesting data and corroborates how often what people say about themselves does not coincide with the material record of what they actually do. William Rathje (1992), who won an American Association for the Advancement of Science Award for his *Tucson Garbage Project*, showed, for example, that what US citizens describe when asked about their consumption habits does not correspond with the contents of the trash cans they keep right outside their houses. He also learned that this does not necessarily make them liars as much as they are unable to recognize some of the things they do. My training as an archaeologist has persuaded me that, if we want to know what people are really like, we should consider not what they say but what they do.

An entire portion of our own behavior is simply unacknowledged by our conscious and explicit discourse, either because it lacks social recognition or because it represents parts of ourselves which we ourselves would rather not be reminded of. As a result, this part can be *denied* in the sense that it cannot be seen and remains unknown to those who are displaying it in front of our eyes. It must be understood that people in these situations are not lying but that they simply fail to recognize what they are doing. Throughout this text, when I use the word *denial*, I shall not be referring to the act of saying that we do not know something which we actually do know but to really not knowing and to being truly unaware of doing what we are doing.

Here, I propose adopting a prehistorian's gaze—i.e., focusing on long-term processes that start at the origins—and an archaeologists' gaze (a careful observation of what subjects actually do) to understand certain aspects of the social order in which we live, particularly to the relations between men and women. This order has been called *patriarchal* because it is the result of an entire historical trajectory defined by male domination and the subordination of women, a power relationship which has survived as the social norm to this very day. In the following pages, I shall try to expose some of the keys that explain the logic behind the patriarchal order but, especially, by trying to unravel its logic, to help us all combat this subordination.

1.2

All societies produce their own truth, which in turn sustains the powers guiding each particular society, a circular procedure which Foucault (1977: 14) referred to as a "regime of truth": "truth is linked by a circular relation to systems of power which produce and sustain it, and to effects of power which it induces and which redirect it." Power sustains itself because society considers *true* the principles it is based on, which in turn causes those who ascribe to these principles to attain power, thus reinforcing a particular regime of truth. In our society, "The 'truth' lies in scientific discourse and the institutions that produce it" (ibid.: also Adorno and Horkheimer 2002: 2), so if we want to untangle the logic that guides our social order, we must ask ourselves about the specific relationship between science and the power logic that characterizes it. Interestingly, although both physics and the natural and social sciences have been seeing alternative and critical formulations develop for quite some time, the most socially accepted stereotype of scientific rationality is still modeled on the methods of seventeenth-century physics (Midgley 2004: 31). These used to compare the functioning and movement of physical particles with those of a machine, an analogy used to describe any organism made of those particles. The human body itself was included among these organisms by Descartes, and although the French philosopher and scientist excluded the human mind from the analogy, other authors extended it to this domain too. This led to an appraisal as *true* of accounts of human society that endorsed mechanistic and computable machine-like behavior (ibid.: 49). Such a reductionist way of understanding society (which we know as *positivism*) not only leaves out human beings' emotional dimension but also the very complexity of the interactions that make up the entire universe. I shall start with the latter.

Understanding the universe in its complexity is a task in many ways opposed to the standard procedures of positive science. These typically include analyzing discrete and separate elements, giving detailed accounts of their features and traits, and classifying, computing, and measuring their components. However, researchers in all fields (including physics) have, over a good number of years, come to consider it a mistake to apply this type of approach to the study of any given dynamic, arguing that the form or characteristics of any one of a system's elements is the result of its complex interaction with all the rest, thus introducing a dimension of *disorder* which the trivial model of the machine could not possibly account for.[1] The dissociations deployed by positive science should therefore be abandoned in order to understand the processes that these elements participate in. In the case of human phenomena, these dissociations include the following dichotomies: subject-object, society-person, culture-nature, body-mind, dominator-dominated, etc.[2] To explain this better, I will turn to an example I am particularly familiar with: the subject-object interaction.

Traditional archaeology has always (and to this day continues to do so) interpreted objects as passive products, generated by societies, which were all seen as invariably guided by the same logic (in turn assumed to be identical to the logic guiding archaeologists themselves). Within traditional archaeological frameworks, all an archaeologist needed in order to be able to *explain* any given society would be access to and thorough descriptions of either the objects or the raw economic data

---

[1] Morín (2002) points out that, although the universe is the product of what he calls a "dialogic of order and disorder" (p. 329), positive sciences have considered that "organization is a function of order, pure and simple" (p. 330), likening the (nontrivial) functioning of society to that of an artificial (trivial) machine, which would differ from it in that it doesn't tolerate disorder and would cease to operate if disorder were ever to appear (p.331). The "living machine," on the other hand, finds, precisely within this disorder, the possibilities for freedom, creativity, and change (pp. 331–2).

[2] Many authors have highlighted the difficulty of understanding different types of processes if their integrating parts are isolated. See, for example, Elias (1991b), Morin (2002), Viveiros de Castro (1996), Descola (1996, 2013), Haraway (1985), Callon (1991), Strathern (1988), or, more broadly, entire schools of thought such as structuralist, post-structuralist, postcolonial, decolonial, and feminist perspectives.

about each particular society. More recent archaeological research, however, has begun to prove the impossibility of separating the subjects from the objects of cultural analysis: if the objects from different cultures vary, this is because the people who make them are different from each other too. From this other perspective, it becomes clear that people make material culture as much as material culture makes people. That is, we are the way we are because we use certain objects, and it is because of our own particular way of being that we make certain objects and not others.[3]

I will try to illustrate this with an example from my own travel experience in the part of the world I know and love best, Latin America: traveling by bus around Latin-American indigenous regions means immersing oneself in a social milieu that can hardly be defined through individualizing features. Therefore, we very rarely find individualized seats inside these buses but instead continuous benches to seat far more people than could ever be dreamed of by our compartmentalized Western imagination, with its resistance to physical contact with strangers. Also, living with these indigenous peoples, one will quickly find that food is rarely served on individualized plates but in collective recipients, where each person takes what they wish, using their fingers and not cutlery. None of this is even imaginable in the individualized culture of the urban European context I live in, in Madrid, where each individual seat is clearly separated on public transport and where eating together requires pristine hygienic measures of interpersonal separation. I want to highlight that not only do we produce individualized objects as a result of our individuation but, also, that through their everyday use, we become more and more individuated ourselves, so that, in the future, we will continue to produce increasingly individualized objects, which will, in turn, further deepen the logic of this social trend. In this respect, think of the transformations of personal relationships that have taken place over the past 20 years and how utterly inconceivable they would be without the material devices that are their vehicles (cellphones, computers, etc.), or remember the changes undergone by screens on airplanes, in parallel to the increase in our own individuality: until a few years ago, economy-class passengers had a single entertainment option, shown on one big screen, which was then divided into a number of smaller screens distributed among the seats. The latest aircrafts, however, have equipped each seat with a small TV screen so that each passenger can choose from a wide range of options, bringing their own personal desires into play, rather than forcing them to adapt to those of airline programmers. The point is that the passenger is not only *able to* choose but also *made to* choose, making them stop and think to try to identify these desires, which routinely and unconsciously reinforces their individuality (another case in point is the experience of

---

[3] Recent trends in archaeology (such as symmetrical archaeology) and contemporary material culture studies have been quite insistent on this point. See, for example, González Ruibal et al. (2011), Hernando and González Ruibal (2011), Olsen (2010), Holbraad (2009), Knappett and Malafouris (eds.) (2008), or Witmore (2007), among others.

trying to make a simple choice and pick *just any* quick snack at some US restaurant chains[4]).

The point I am trying to make is that material culture is not a merely passive instrument of culture but that, quite on the contrary, it is one of its most powerful means of construction, so both are closely knit and mutually determined. As a consequence, the study of material culture will always be highly revealing about those aspects which societies do not reflect on or state explicitly. Material culture could thus be said to express profound cultural traits, the cultural unconscious. And while it would be impossible to study people of the same terms as we use for present societies, we may conclude that, if past people had different material culture, this is because they themselves were different and they had different ways of understanding the world and different ways of creating their identities.

This same impossibility of separating different parts from the whole affects any other interaction. We often think of reality as a whole, all constituent elements of which could be separated like a machine, but in actual fact, these parts owe their very existence to their constant codetermination and interaction. Let us turn now, for example, to the relationship between person and society. Traditionally, there used to be two positions about this: there were those who prioritized society in the shaping of a person's character and those who prioritized people as determining factors in the characteristics of their societies. Today, the idea that neither side of the spectrum can be taken as a separate entity is gaining momentum, and both elements begin to be perceived as two sides of the same coin.

In his famous book *Civilization and Its Discontents*, Sigmund Freud (1986: 144) established "a far-reaching similarity" between the "individual" and civilization. According to Freud, both expressed similar phenomena, which meant they were subject to comparable pathologies. Still, he warned about the risks of trying to apply similar cures to both, as he saw these as "mere analogies." Despite Freud's complete ignorance of the most basic ethnological data and the profoundly evolutionist foundations of his (and his society's) thought, this perception of the relationship between person and culture can be traced in some of the most recent trends of thought about human dynamics. In fact, the links are now seen as even more profound, for, unlike Freud, who spoke of a mere *analogy*, several authors (whom I personally identify with) have, since the 1990s, taken up the concept of a *fractal* relationship.[5] These authors also emphasize the impossibility of separating person from culture, as they consider both instances to be the simultaneous expression of the same process at

---

[4] Elias (1991a, b: 121) already referred to the obligation of choice—and not just the possibilities—that individuality entails: individuals "not only *can* but *must* be more selfsufficient. On this point, they have no choice."

[5] This concept and its use in the social sciences can be traced in Hernando and González Ruibal (2011: 14). Its foundations were laid by Wagner (1991), Abraham (1993), MacWhinney (1990), Haraway (1985), and Strathern (1990). Recently, such authors as Viveiros de Castro (2001) or Kelly (2005) have applied it to the analysis of Amazonian groups. Leaving aside some of these complex interpretations, I shall limit my own use of the concept to considering that the "individual and group are false alternatives doubly so implicated because each implies the other" (Wagner 1991: 162) and that their relation is one of scale and not determination, as explained in the text.

different scales and see the differentiation between the whole and its parts as completely senseless. If capitalist society, for example, is defined by certain economic or social traits, this is because the people who make it up interact in certain ways and not others. This, in turn, is due to the fact that their subjectivity is modeled accordingly, causing them to interact in particular ways. In a similar way, an *egalitarian* hunter-gatherer society not only implies a certain form of socioeconomic organization but also a certain modeling of its members' subjectivities, and so on and so forth (we shall elaborate further on this point below). Therefore, the characteristics of any given society are nothing but an expression of the specific way of *being a person* adopted by those who constitute it, that is, their *identity mode*.

These ideas continue a trend long represented by such authors as Bourdieu (1977), Giddens (1984), Elias (1994), or Morin (2002), who proposed a constant interaction and codetermination between society and people. In these authors' view, by the use of its language, norms, prohibitions, or knowledge, all societies gradually come to shape each one of the members born within it in a specific way of being a person. In turn and due to the particular way in which they have been brought up, people generate new dynamics that will slowly come to define and change their societies. To give a very well-known example: having been brought up in a specific social context, with its particular dynamics, needs, attitudes, and potentialities, Mark Zuckerberg conceived the idea of Facebook, which, while satisfying all of these needs, also created a number of new trends which are currently transforming society itself. In the same way as we could not possibly understand Facebook without Zuckerberg's cultural context, we will not be able to understand current and future trends in the socialization of generations to come without Facebook. A certain social order and its members' subjectivities constitute two levels at which the same structure can be observed.

1.3

Our society is characterized by the shared belief that our own group is stronger than the rest because we have developed *reason* and repressed *emotions* more than any other group. This is not only reflected in the social discourse that models us, enshrined as *the truth* ever since the time of the Enlightenment, but also in the type of science which, to this day, continues to provide the most widespread model of explanation (the *positivist* model); it also informs the identity of men in the highest positions of authority, where they continue to produce this discourse, triggering an endless feedback between social order and subjectivity. All of these different scales reflect the same dynamics in our relationships with the world.

As has already been analyzed in considerable depth by several authors, once positive science began to pretend that emotions are not an integral part of knowledge, it became impossible to reincorporate this dimension into the dynamics under study and to envision human relationships and behavior in their full nature and complexity.[6] While emotions could be seen as the element of *disorder* in social interaction, prevailing models in the social sciences and humanities have paradigmatically contemplated only those ordered and predictable elements which could fit into the model of the machine. The resulting images these models cast project an image of society as guided by mechanisms which are not only seen as controllable but also as potentially subject to design and planning.

This reductionist assessment of human phenomena slowly came into being at the same time as society itself became increasingly complex from the socioeconomic point of view and while it was developing science and technology. By the eighteenth century, it had become the basis of social discourse, in what became known as the Enlightenment. Emotions became definitively *denied* as a determining component of the *ideal* human behavior, which, in order to guarantee order, emancipation, and *progress*, should only be based on reason: the more human beings turned to reason, the freer, more emancipated and powerful they would become. And yet, far from bringing about liberation and emancipation, the implementation of this enlightened project has caused increasing personal unrest and a very dangerous commodification of both the human and the nonhuman world. Abhorrent peaks of monstrous rationalization have been reached (such as the Nazi holocaust), as well as situations of injustice, inequality, and suffering which appear to defy all conscious and planned design, as if reality slipped through our fingers without us being able to explain why. Confused and disoriented, we stagger toward a future that seems increasingly unplanned, un-liberating, and incompatible with humanitarian values and princi ples. In their famous work *Dialectic of Enlightenment*, Adorno and Horkheimer argued that this contradiction between the Enlightenment's predictions and actual historical developments was rooted in the *type* of reason being used by society. In their opinion, the Enlightenment project could only be fulfilled by an abandonment of purely instrumental Kantian reason in favor of a *critical reason* which would take into consideration the ultimate aims and consequences of actions, that is, the morality of acts, which instrumental reason had relegated to obscurantism. Also, Habermas (1984: 66) held that modern Western societies "foster a distorted understanding of rationality, focused on cognitive and instrumental aspects, in this sense, merely particular."

Contemporary criticisms seem to follow similar paths, although, unlike those who preceded them, they clearly state that *denial of the emotional dimension* is one of the key aspects of the problem. Mary Midgley (2004: 127 and 130), for example, argues that the Enlightenment-born notion that the individual is essentially "a will using and intellect," capable of generating thought in an "impartial, uninvolved, rational, and impersonal" way, is one of the many prevailing myths in our culture, for it is impossible to set apart reason and emotion. This is the very conclusion that many recent neurological studies are increasingly arriving at, as they grasp that human cognition and thought are the result of an inseparable combination of both

---

[6] Migley (2004: 206) rightly observes that for most researchers, "to study subjective phenomena is the same as being subjective," which is as wrong as thinking that "the study of folly must be a foolish study or that the study of evil conducts an evil one."

domains: reason and emotion (Damasio 1994). In fact, these studies propose that it is emotions and our capacity for empathy that allow an assessment of the type of rational logic to be used in each situation, in order to arrive at the greatest possible efficacy. In fact, people who, as a result of brain damage, become incapable of activating the neurological centers that connect them to emotions make the most disastrous and life-endangering decisions. As Edgar Morin (2002: 337) pointed out for social systems, in these cases, rationality operates within "a closed logical system, incapable of seeing reality."

The arguments put forth in this book develop these same ideas: the reason why the auspicious future of emancipation predicted by the Enlightenment is falling apart before our frightened and unbelieving eyes is because it was designed around *a false belief that has survived to this day as one of the pillars of our social order, of classical science, and of the identity of the men* who (in a fractal relationship) are in command of society. This conviction is that the individual can be conceived of as set apart from community and that reason can exist separately from emotion; that the more individuated a person becomes, the less they will need to cultivate community bonds to feel safe, and that the more they use reason to establish relationships with the world, the less they will resort to emotions. This notion, which has—ever since the Enlightenment period— structured the ideals of our social system and which reassures the personal security of most men in positions of power, is, as I will try to prove in the following pages, based on a fantasy. I have called it *the fantasy of individuality*.

It could be objected that the idea that emotions play a relevant role in relationships of knowledge has been accepted in postmodern quarters for quite some time. While this is definitely the case, the importance afforded by postmodern thought to *subjectivity* is such that knowledge has been reduced to a simple *narrative*, always mediated by the particular conditions of each subject, precluding the establishment of objective conditions for validation. As a consequence, postmodern discourse fails to constitute a useful tool of social critique, a task which I consider indispensable among those of us who have the privilege of devoting our lives to intellectual reflection.

The arguments I shall develop in the following pages steer clear of postmodern ones and join the critical line of what might be called a *theory of complexity*, a trend present today among researchers of all scientific disciplines. I base my arguments on the principle that knowledge must be subject to validation and can therefore be considered objective while escaping the shortcomings of *positive* science and its identification of human dynamics with the ordered, predictable, and controllable mechanisms of machines. The arguments that follow take into consideration not just the level of reason and recognized and conscious behavior but also the disorder of both emotions and *denied* and unconscious behavior.[7]

---

[7] Damasio (1994: 146) recognizes that neurology envisages "a vast domain of nonconscious processes, some part of which is amenable to psychological explanation and some part of which is not."

The difference between these arguments and those already developed along similar lines is that, through them, I will try to prove that *the belief that the individual can be autonomous from their community and that reason can be autonomous from emotion is intrinsically, insolubly, and directly related to the need to subordinate women*. I argue that it was precisely because the importance of emotional bonds was denied that this subordination became (and continues to be) indispensable. In this sense, it could be said that the Enlightenment elevated to the category of truth, the very basis of what is known as the *patriarchal order*.

This means that the reasons why the social order has been built historically upon the subordination of women are neither conscious nor explicit but that they belong to the realm of the *denied*. This is why it is not enough (although it is obviously necessary) to develop our arguments exclusively on the level of the recognized and the conscious—the level of reason—if we are to develop a truly emancipatory social project based on the equality of rights for both sexes. While it is important and necessary to change laws and guarantee that increasing numbers of women gain access to power, inequality will continue to prevail unless it is confronted on another level, by trying to bring to the light precisely what social discourse *denies*, what people do without even noticing that they are doing. Only on this level can we find the ultimate cause of that inequality, the reason that explains, for example, why some men whose discourse is clearly in favor of gender equality are capable of sustaining unequal relationships (perhaps full of affection but profoundly unequal in terms of power) in their personal lives. These men often fail to recognize the power relations which are inherent to their relationships and attribute them to necessary complementarities, certain *feminine* qualities which they find particularly attractive, or other similar *reasons*. The real reason behind the contradictions between their discourse and their personal lives is that neither these contradictions nor the power relation inherent to inequality is visible to them or susceptible to transformation through rational argumentation. I therefore consider that in order to struggle for equality, it is not enough to ask these men to use their reason, as the relationship of domination is in no way based on the reasons that (intelligent) men insist on defending but on emotions which they cannot understand and therefore *deny*. This fact, which, in my opinion, becomes visible only by focusing on what is done, and not on what is said, must be revealed in order to unveil the mechanisms governing men's domination over women.

1.4

The main argument of this book, the axis it moves along, is that the Western world has gradually built for itself a logical order defined by an increased *dissociation between reason and emotion*, idealizing reason as the sole basis for security and human survival and *denying* emotional bonds even the slightest value in sustaining such security. I shall argue that, on the contrary, the feeling of belonging to a group, upheld by emotional bonds between its members, is not only vital but also constitutes the *only* indispensable strategy for all human beings to feel secure about their capacity to survive: this can be generated by activating exclusively emotional mechanisms (hunter-gatherers' myths) and without any rational ones, but it cannot be generated conversely, i.e., through rational mechanisms and without emotional ones. Nonetheless, the Western world slowly came to construe a social discourse where, as the mechanisms of reason developed (scientific knowledge, technological control, personal power), emotional resources (such as the feeling of belonging to a group) were increasingly veiled; while never ceasing to exist, they were simply increasingly unacknowledged and made invisible.

In order to *convince itself* that it does not need something that is in fact indispensable (the emotional connection that generates a feeling of belonging) and to elevate this appearance of things to the status of *truth*, the social order came to develop a number of strategies, including—though not exclusively—the domination of women. Here, I will develop the idea that men have not had the need to dominate women simply because they are women but because women came to *specialize* in sustaining group bonds, a security mechanism which was indispensable for men, but one whose recognition was inversely proportional to that afforded to reason as a means of gaining control and power over the world. And the single reason this happened in this particular way was that, as we shall see, both security mechanisms (the one based on emotion and the one based on reason) operate through quite contradictory ontological and psychological dynamics. There is no *essence* in anyone's sex that can explain the power relations which have characterized relationships between men and women throughout most of our history. I therefore consider that in order to understand these power relations, we must undertake a thorough assessment of the socialization dynamics which have come to define them.

1.5

Understanding the making of the idea that reason can be autonomous—which is nothing short of understanding the making of a social order characterized by gender inequality (what is known as the *patriarchal order*)—can not only help us liberate women but also men. While it is true that they currently occupy most positions of power, men have come to do so by hiding and repressing within themselves the very (emotional) dimension that has caused them to conceal and repress women. In need of emotional bonds, men have prevented women from becoming individuated so that these women could maintain emotional bonds with the world for them. In this sense, I think it would be worth substituting the term *patriarchal order* for the term *dissociated reason-emotion order*. This would allow us to understand that if some women gain access to power without questioning the logic that sustains it, they shall not transform but rather reinforce the social order they believe to be combatting, thus perpetuating the subordination of most other women. The struggle for equality should not be restricted to multiplying the number of women in power but should also contribute to unveiling and transforming the logic that has characterized this power so far (political, scientific, economic, etc.). Also, discussions about a *dissociated reason-emotion order* would help men understand, for example, that the struggle for equal rights between men and women is not restricted to reclaiming women's rights but also pursues their rights to stop *denying* the transcendental importance that emotions and bonds have for men themselves, thus liberating them from a form of socialization which forces them to repress their emotions.[8]

1.6

By no means is this book intended as an erudite essay. Even if I tried, I would probably fail to produce one, but it is still far from my intentions. I shall limit myself to trying to put forth a number of heterodox and multidisciplinary reflections about the *problem* of inequality between men and women in our society and its relation to the way in which reason has been prioritized and favored over emotions in the prevailing discourses which we, as a society, continue to reinforce. Although I think that several of the arguments I will defend here could be applied to other cultures, I shall focus exclusively on our own, as I find it indispensable to understand specific historical contexts in order to be able to sustain any kind of statement about them.

In order to buttress the theoretical arguments of this book, I have drawn on historical (and prehistoric) data from our own cultural trajectory and combined them with speculative theoretical reasoning. While explaining the origins and development of the gender inequality that characterizes our social order constitutes a necessarily speculative dare, I have supported my arguments on the empirical data available both about modern Western society and about other less-complex contemporary societies. I have based my speculations on ethnological and ethnoarchaeological data, both from bibliographical searches at several US universities (UCLA, Berkeley, Chicago, and Harvard) and from my own field projects (especially in Brazil and Guatemala), as well as on archaeological and historical data obtained by others.

The bibliography in this book is far from comprehensive, as it would be impossible to take into consideration all the elements involved in the processes described. These would have to be observed from all possible points of view, considering the

---

[8] Way (2011) analyzes how the process of socialization makes US adolescents go from openly recognizing the importance of emotions to denying them when they begin to feel like adults. Both she and Carol Gilligan (1990) talk about an increasing "crisis of connection" undergone by adolescents and impelled by a social discourse which identifies male "maturity" with "emotional independence and stoicism" (ibid.: 268). This causes them to suffer in a way which they can still recognize at the start of adolescence but which they cannot possibly express at later stages in their lives, once they have identified with the system.

In fact, nowadays there are several support groups created by men who struggle to escape what they call a hegemonic masculinity (Connell 1995). A number of different aspects of contemporary discussions about the concept of masculinity can be reviewed in Carabí and Armengol (eds.) (2008), Lomas (ed.) (2002), or Bonino (1999), among others.

countless factors affecting the construing and development of our society. It would be ridiculous to even consider this as a possibility, especially if we acknowledge the need to study interactions and not isolated elements. I have therefore focused on studying some of these interactions from a very partial point of view, recognizing the insufficiency of these very pages from the start. I shall restrict my efforts to analyzing the way in which male and female identities have been forged throughout our history, in order to understand the relationship between these processes, the growing power of men and the increasing value ascribed to reason over emotion.

1.7

In the following pages, I will focus on trying to prove that the *dissociation of reason and emotion* is the key to the so-called patriarchal order and analyze how the fact that men and women have been made to follow historically disparate identity paths has resulted in their discovery of different ways of construing modern individuality. In order to do so, I will constantly return to the very flexible term *identity*. By this term, I mean every person's ideas about who they are and about the nature of the world around them. For most people, identity does not operate on a reflexive level, which means that they rarely even think about, much less try to define it intellectually. It is simply something they perform. We simply behave in one way or another, and, depending on this behavior, we establish certain types of relationships, feel more or less powerful or secure toward the world, devote higher or lower levels of abstraction to considering its dynamics, and give more or less importance to creating bonds or belonging to collectives or groups. Generally speaking, most people are so unaware that they actually *have an* identity that they mistakenly take for granted that the rest of the world population perceives the world in exactly the same way as they do. They tend to assume that if others should take different decisions from their own or if the same facts cause different emotions or reactions in them, this is because these others are mistaken or because they are ignorant, unintelligent, or underdeveloped, as it seems clear to them that the only way or at least the best way of relating to different phenomena is of course their own.

However, we human beings display a very wide range of different identities, necessities, and assessments of the same facts. Even a single person's identity may change in the course of their life. As children, our identity is initially modeled on the ways of behaving and seeing the world that have been handed down to us by our parents (identity comes from *idem*, which means *the same*), who assist us in gradually shaping our worldview to fit in the social group we are a part of (Jenkins 1996: 4–5). But identity is also always a dynamic and interactive process whose main function is to generate in us the idea that we are safe in the world and that we are capable of surviving in it, so our identity can be transformed by changes in our ability to control the world around us.

There are many different types of mechanisms through which we can shape our ideas of what the world means to us and of our position in it. Elsewhere

(Hernando 2002), I have analyzed the fundamental structure of identity in some detail and how it is basically shaped by the way in which we perceive and represent space and time. Therefore, I shall not be referring here to that level of analysis and will merely highlight a certain aspect of the mechanisms of identity which is particularly relevant to understand the fantasies underpinning the patriarchal order. This aspect is the need (shared by all human beings) to feel linked by bonds with a group to reassure themselves about their own ability to survive.

1.8

The question of whether the first representatives of our species *Homo sapiens* and the modern culture that continues to characterize us to this day appeared simultaneously or not is still the subject of some debate (McBrearty and Brooks 2000). However, all researchers seem to agree that toward 50–40,000 BC, a new type of behavior was displayed by human groups as they began to spread from Africa to the rest of the world and who first occupied America and Oceania. Among the many traits of their modern culture were symbolic abilities. This means that, unlike previous representatives of the *Homo* genus (*habilis, ergaster, erectus, antecessor, neanderthal*, etc.), *sapiens* could endow the world with a meaning which was not inherent to it, a meaning that transcended and enriched it: *sapiens* could imagine Gods protecting them and spirits accompanying them—explanations that put them at ease and rendered significant a world perceived to have incredible complexity, thanks to their newly acquired greater intelligence. From our very emergence as a species, we *sapiens* have never given up this quest for meaning, this struggle against perplexity, and the anguish that might overcome us in the face of our own sheer minuteness, insufficiency, and essential impotence before a world that everywhere surpasses us and daunts us. We have never given up on that need to inscribe into the world a logic that allows us to think we know where we are and that we are in sufficient control of the circumstances that we live in. It is the quiet and unconscious response to this demand, the primal idea, indistinguishable from what the very world means to each one of us that constitutes the very basis of identity.

Identity mechanisms fulfil the function of eliciting an image of ourselves as capable of surviving in a world which would otherwise appear too overwhelming, and so, each group creates group identity in different ways, depending on their real material capacity for control (later on we will look into the personal scale). And yet all of them invariably do so by entertaining the same idea: that their own particular group has the necessary keys to be able to survive better than the rest.

In order to construe this fantasy, the human mind considers *reality* to be made up exclusively of those phenomena which the group can control or understand sufficiently and selects these phenomena by arranging them in space and time (Elias 1992; Hernando 2002). This means that anything that cannot be arranged into these parameters will fail to be integrated into what each human group calls the reality they live in. Think, for example, of the sheer impossibility of the modern Western mind to even fathom *what lies beyond the universe*. The boundaries we set upon our own *imaginable* worlds are equivalent to those that prevent a group of Amazonian hunter-gatherers from integrating the idea of, say, Europe into their mind-set. Because these societies do not use maps to order space, the portion of reality that lies outside of walking distances transcends what they can arrange mentally. To them, Europe is as excluded from what can be conceived as the idea of *beyond the universe* is to our Western mind. Each group creates for itself a world which fits their own ability to control it, and they will place within the limits of the imaginable only those phenomena which they are capable of ordering and conceiving of in an organized fashion.

As well as the *construction of the world*, all human groups have used two strategies of reassurance and legitimation to develop social discourses that invariably assert the same idea: our own group is the only holder of the keys to survival, so we can consider ourselves *chosen* to survive among all the rest. Within our own group, they would seem to say, we can rest assured, forget about our fears, and deny that we even have them, as only *we* are protected by the instance that governs the rest of the world. The following are the two main strategies:

(a) The strategy of creating a legitimating discourse (Hernando 2006), of which there are two types: *myth*, which is typically found among groups with little control over their material life conditions—and who therefore reject the risks implied by change—and *history*, a substitute for myth as the discourse of social legitimation in those groups beyond a certain level of socioeconomic complexity and technological control, where change comes to be considered as a precondition for survival. Both discourses reassure the groups that have generated and believe in them of the same idea that everyone's own group is the *chosen* one (by God or fate) to survive.

(b) The strategy of engaging (through emotional bonds) with the group we belong to—which I discuss in this book and which is perhaps even more necessary than the first. Each and every one of us needs to feel that we are not an isolated instance of existence, but part of a greater, much stronger and powerful entity, an entity mighty enough to make us feel strong in the face of a universe which would otherwise appear threatening and daunting: we all *need to feel* part of the group we belong to. It is simply impossible to renounce this need for belonging, as isolation would do nothing but reveal our individual minuteness and incapacity to cope with the enormity of the universe around us. Understandably, this need becomes more explicit and recognized the less material control there is over lived circumstances. Think, for example, of hunter-gatherers, or of so-called *youth tribes*, made up of teenagers who need to feel powerful in contexts over which they have no control, at an age when their insecurity in the face of the world makes itself particularly manifest. In both cases, individuals only feel secure insofar as they are part of a larger group that provides them safety, so, as we shall see below, group members unify their appearance. This means that the less material control groups have over the world around them, the more they recognize their need for bonds with other group members, as these ensure a feeling of control and of one's ability to survive in it.

The main point is that, historically, at the same time as technological control rose—a process which cannot possibly be dissociated from the multiplication of functions and work specialization—the need to belong was increasingly denied, until, by the seventeenth century, the concept of person had become identified with that of the *individual* (Mauss 1968; Elias 1991a, b: 161). That century saw a majority of men in the social group begin to conceive themselves as *isolated instances that could be separated from the group they belonged to*, as they no longer considered the key to their strength and safety to reside in their belonging to a group but in their particular ability to reason (*cogito ergo sum*). And yet, this is quite simply a *fantasy*. If human beings really perceived themselves in an isolated way, their own impotence before the world would dawn on them so strikingly that they could not possibly survive. Individuality mistakenly attributes each isolated one of us a security and power that we actually lack, a fact which would become evident if we ever had to really cope with the universe on an individual basis. I therefore believe that understanding the way in which this fantasy has been construed so successfully and without betraying its own artificial character means understanding the keys of the profound inconsistency, the fantasy that lies beneath the discourse sustaining our social order. It also means understanding the two distinct trajectories that have defined the separate processes of individuation of men and women in the Western World: the former has been progressive and gradual, while the latter has been sudden and abrupt and has only come about in modernity. It also means understanding the differences that have come to characterize the individuality of men and women to this day. Finally, the distinct trajectories of men and women's individuation explain why the latter provides the identity mode which, in my opinion, ought to be followed if we want to construct a society guided by equal rights for all its members.

I shall devote the following pages to all of this. First I shall briefly review the origins and meaning of the concept of gender, to turn later to an analysis of the information available about our own origins as a species. To a prehistorian's gaze, only from this starting point can the rest of the process be fully understood.

References

Abraham, R. H. (1993). Human fractals. The arabesque in our mind. *Visual Anthropology Review,* 9(1), 52–55.

Adorno, T.W. & Horkheimer, M. (2002)[1987]. *Dialectic of enlightenment : Philosophical fragments.* Stanford: Stanford University Press.

Bonino, L. (1999). Varones, género y salud mental: Deconstruyendo la "normalidad" masculina. In M. Segarra & Á. Carabí (Eds.), *Nuevas masculinidades* (pp. 41–64). Barcelona: Icaria.

Bourdieu, P. (1977). *Outline of a theory of practice.* Cambridge: Cambridge University Press.

Callon, M. (1991). Techno-economic networks and irreversibility. In J. Law (Ed.), *A sociology of monsters. Sociological review monograph* (pp. 132–164). Londres: Routledge.

Carabí, Á., & Armengol, J. M. (Eds.). (2008). *La masculinidad a debate.* Barcelona: Icaria.

Connell, R. W. (1995). *Masculinities.* Berkeley: University of California Press.

Damasio, A. (1994). *Descartes' error.* New York: G.P. Putnam.

Descola, P. (1996). Constructing natures: Symbolic ecology and social practice. In P. Descola & G. Pálsson (Eds.), *Nature and society. Anthropological perspectives* (pp. 82–102). Routledge: Londres.
Descola, P. (2013). *Beyond nature and culture*. Chicago: University of Chicago Press.
Elias, N. (1991a). *The society of individuals*. London: Basil Blackweell.
Elias, N. (1991b). On human beings and their emotions: A process-sociology essay. In M. Featherstone, M. Hepworth, & B. S. Turner (Eds.), *The body. Social process and cultural theory* (pp. 103–125). London: Sage.
Elias, N. (1992). *Time: An essay*. Oxford: Basil Blackwell.
Elías, N. (1994). *The civilizing process. The history of manners and state formation and civilization*. Oxford: Blackwell.
Foucault, M. (1977). The political function of the intellectual. *Radical Philosophy, 17*, 12–14.
Freud, S. (1986). Civilization and its discontents (1930)[1929]. In: *The standard edition of the complete psychological works of sigmund freud. XXI* (pp. 64–145). London: Hogarth Press.
Giddens, A. (1984). *The constitution of society. Outline of the theory of structuration*. Berkeley and Los Ángeles: California University Press.
Gilligan, C. (1990). Teaching Shakespeare' sister: Notes from the underground of the female adolescence. In C. Gilligan, N. Lions, & T. Hammer (Eds.), *Making connections: The relational worlds of adolescent girls at Emma Willard School* (pp. 6–29). Cambridge, MA: Harvard University Press.
González Ruibal, A., Hernando, A., & Politis, G. (2011). Ontology of the self and material culture: Arrow-making among the Awá hunter-gatherers (Brasil). *Journal of Anthropological Archaeology, 30*, 1–16.
Habermas, J. (1984). *The theory of communicative action. Volume 1: Reason and the rationalization of society*. Boston: Beacon Press.
Haraway, D. (1985). A manifesto for cyborgs: Science, technology, and socialist feminism in the 1980s. *Socialist Review, 80*, 65–107.
Hernando, A. (2002). *Arqueología de la Identidad*. Madrid: Akal.
Hernando, A. (2006). Arqueología y globalización. El problema de la definición del 'otro' en la postmodernidad. *Complutum, 17*, 221–234.
Hernando, A., & González Ruibal, A. (2011). Fractalidad, materialidad y cultura. Un estudio etnoarqueológico de los Awá-Guajá (Maranhão, Brasil). *Revista Chilena de Antropología, 24*, 9–61.
Holbraad, M. (2009). Ontology, ethnography, archaeology: An afterword on the ontography of things. *Cambridge Archaeological Journal, 19*(3), 431–441.
Jenkins, R. (1996). *Social identity*. Londres y Nueva York: Routledge.
Kelly, J. A. (2005). Fractality and the exchange of perspectives. In M. S. Mosko & F. H. Damon (Eds.), *On the order of chaos. Social anthropology and the science of chaos* (pp. 108–135). Nueva York: Berghahn Books.
Knappett, C., & Malafouris, L. (Eds.). (2008). *Material agency: Towards a non-anthropocentric approach*. Nueva York: Springer-Kluwer.
Lomas, C. (Ed.). (2002). *Todos los hombres son iguales? Identidad masculina y cambios sociales*. Barcelona: Paidós.
MacWhinney, W. (1990). Fractals cast no shadows. *IS Journal, 5*(1), 9–12.
Mauss, M. (1968)[1950]. A category of the human spirit. *Psychoanalitical Review 55*, 457–481.
McBrearty, S., & Brooks, A. (2000). The revolution that wasn't: A new interpretation of the origin of modern human behavior. *Journal of Human Evolution, 39*, 453–563.
Midgley, Mary (2004). *The myths we live by*. Londres/New York: Routledge Classics.
Morin, E. (2002). The epistemology of complexity. In D. F. Schnitman & J. Schnitman (Eds.), *New paradigms, culture and subjectivity* (pp. 325–340). Cresskill: Hampton Press.
Olsen, B. (2010). *In defense of things: Archaeology and the ontology of objects*. Lanham: AltaMira.
Rathje, W. L. (1992). *Rubbish!: The archaeology of garbage*. New York: Harpercollins.
Strathern, M. (1988). *The gender of the gift. Problems with women and problems with society in Melanesia*. Berkeley: University of California Press.

References

Strathern, M. (1990). *Partial connections,* asad (Special Publication N 3). University Press of America.

Viveiros de Castro, E. (1996). Os pronomes cosmológicos e o perspectivismo ameríndio. *Mana, 2*(2), 115–144.

Viveiros de Castro, E. (2001). GUT feelings about Amazonia: Potential affinity and the construction of sociality. In L. M. Rival & N. L. Whitehead (Eds.), *Beyond the visible and the material. The amerindianization of society in the work of Peter Rivière* (pp. 19–43). Oxford: Oxford University Press.

Wagner, R. (1991). The fractal person. In M. Godelier & M. Strathern (Eds.), *Big men and great men. Personifications of power in Melanesia* (pp. 159–173). Cambridge: Cambridge University Press.

Way, N. (2011). *Deep secrets. Boys' friendships and the crisis of connection.* Cambridge: Harvard University Press.

Witmore, C. L. (2007). Symmetrical archaeology: Excerpts of a manifesto. *World Archaeology, 39*(4), 546–562.

Chapter 2
Sex and Gender

The term *gender* has permeated common speech so thoroughly that it has become part of everyday language. It seems as if it had always been there and as if everyone used it to refer to the same things. However, this term can designate a wide range of ideas (Scott 1986; Cobo 2005), with very different theoretical, political, and methodological connotations. And although some authors still treat it as an exclusively grammatical concept and define it as a mere "correspondence" (see, e.g., Roca 2005: 25), the term *gender* is generally used "as a way of referring to the social organization of the relationships between the sexes" (Scott 1986: 1053).

About the term's origins, it is worth pointing out that, while in French and Spanish it has traditionally been used almost exclusively to refer to grammatical differences, in English (where grammatical gender is practically irrelevant), the term *gender* began to be used to refer to masculinity and femininity as early as the fourteenth century.[1] In fact, the sex-gender word pair seems to have evolved alongside other opposing pairs where one of the terms comes from either Latin or French and the other from Saxon, expressing physical *vs* symbolic or concrete *vs* abstract values of the same concept: other examples of these would be *dark vs obscure*, *deep vs profound*, or *shallow vs superficial*.[2] So, when it was taken up by John Money in 1955, the term *gender* spread rapidly and easily within English and from there to all other languages.

John Money was a US psychiatrist from the Psychiatry and Pediatrics Department of the Johns Hopkins Hospital (Baltimore, Maryland), who was put in charge of defining what were then called "hermaphrodite"—and now "intersex" babies' sexes. In his opinion (and in that of the greater part of society), it was essential to define a person's sex if they were to enjoy an adapted and psychically healthy life, for—as has been critically pointed out by Queer Theory (Butler 2004)—conforming to this norm was seen as a prerequisite of social recognition. As he explored the

---

[1] According to the Oxford English Dictionary.
[2] I am grateful to philologist José Manuel Bueso for this information.

issue in depth, Money isolated five biological components (Money 1965: 11), the interplay of which defined each person's sex:

(a) Genetic sex: determined by X and Y chromosomes
(b) Hormonal sex: the balance between estrogens and androgens
(c) Gonadal sex: the presence of testicles or ovaries
(d) Internal reproductive organ morphology
(e) External reproductive organ morphology

In principle, most people present aligned orientations of these five components, so we are born with a sex which is defined by society as male or female. But in the case of intersex people (or "hermaphrodites" in Money's time), combinations can vary a great deal, so Money had to decide about the dominating features and enhance them so that each particular person could become a fully accepted member of society. He soon discovered that if he mistakenly began a treatment, for example, to strengthen a female sexual identity, and then, in the course of the baby's physical evolution, their male features developed more, it would become impossible for the person to return to the dominant male identity. Both that person and her entire family and social context had, by this point, become so used to considering them(selves) a woman, that this conviction was of far greater importance than birth, genetic, or any biological traits (ibid.: 12). Although this theory has later been questioned (Haraway 1991: 133; Butler 2004: Chap. 3), the experience caused Money to adopt the term *gender* to refer to a person's "psychosexual identity," which, according to him, becomes fixed in the first few months of a person's life as a result of social interaction. The study of hermaphrodites persuaded Money that society identified a man's body with certain attitudes, beliefs, and potentials and a woman's body with certain others, making each one of them develop differentiated identities as they grew up and fixing traits so strongly and permanently that society could not possibly suspect that they did not "stem from something innate, instinctive, and not subject to postnatal experience and learning" (Money 1965: 12). The concept was later developed into the notion "gender identity" by Robert Stoller, who imported it to psychoanalysis, from his discussions with Ralph Greenson. At the XXIII International Psychoanalytical Congress, published in 1964 (Dio Bleichmar 1998: 79), Stoller used the terms *masculinity* and *femininity* to designate attitudes and not the bodies themselves. In this way, the concept which allows us to differentiate *sex* and *gender* was established and later on imported to the social sciences. Sex refers to the biological fact and the physical characteristics of bodies, whereas gender designates the meanings that each society attaches to this differentiation (Burin 1996: 63).

The question is that the differences between "beliefs, character traits, attitudes, feelings, values, conducts, and activities that differ between men and women" (ibid.: 64)—which define gender—also describe the way in which both sexes are organized in their social relations, so the concept always refers to a relationship. This relationship has been defined as a "power relationship," which, according to many, lies at the very core of the concept of gender (Scott 1986: 1067; Molina Petit 2000: 281). I cannot but agree that close links exist between gender and power in societies with a certain division of functions—and where there are different positions of power—which are previous or separate from modernity. But I would like to keep open the debate about this category and its associations with power, both in so-called *egalitarian* hunter-gatherer societies and in modernity, an issue to which we shall return below.

In any case, the concept of gender always designates a relationship defined by the sexes' mutually complementary social functions. However, researchers often lose sight of this relational aspect and use gender as a synonym for *woman*, simply identifying *gender studies* with *studies about women* or *gender identity* with *women's identity*. Used in this way, the concept of gender does not involve analysis of the power relations in which women are involved, much less any theoretical interpretation of the causes that gave origin to and supported those power relations. Such usage vitiates the analytical and critical capacity that should be inherent in the concept of gender (cf. Cobo 2005; Engelstand 2007).

This already difficult question is further complicated by the fact that, with notably rare exceptions,[3] the concept of gender is considered in such close association to sex that a binary categorization emerges—like the one used by Money himself—, implying that talking about gender nearly always implies talking about the masculine/femenine dichotomy associated to male-/female-sexed bodies. Overall, the concept of gender is so broadly identified with a closed set of traits, that according to some authors (such as Herdt 1994, or Gilchrist 1999: 58–64) we ought to talk about a wider range of genders than those considered by the more traditional—*masculine* and *feminine*—dichotomy. This could include cases where people whose sex is not so well defined adopt nonconventional identities in premodern societies, or when despite having a well-defined sex, they—willingly or forcibly—dress and act according to different rules from those that might be expected of them, bringing about variations. I will try to prove, however, that using the concept of gender as a fixed set of traits prevents us from understanding gender as a dynamic and flexible, and therefore transformable, interplay of identity traits.

Furthermore, associating certain attitudes and behavior patterns strictly to either men or women entails the risk of *naturalizing* them, which in turn leads to reinforcing the patriarchal order instead of combatting it. This could be one of the consequences of, for example, the arguments defended by what is known in Europe as *feminism of sexual difference*, and in the United States as *cultural feminism*, which proposes that gender differences stem from maternity and other alleged *essences* that differentiate the sexes (cf. Posada Kubissa 2007a, b). The problem is that defending the existence of some essential link between *the masculine* and men's sex and between *the feminine* and women's sex only complicates the already difficult struggle for equality, for assuming the existence of natural laws or unalterable essences seems to preclude the kind of dialogue that might support such a struggle.

---

[3] *Queer* theory has questioned the very concept of sex. See Butler (2004). Biologist Fausto-Sterling has also developed interesting studies along the same lines.

The same *naturalization* often seems to underpin theories that explain inequality as a result of women's reproductive capacity, without even explaining the origins of so direct an association between maternity and subordination. Thus, materialist theories, for example (Nicholson 1990; Jónasdóttir 1994; Sanahuja 2002), take for granted men's appropriation of women's reproductive labor or the sexual objectification of women by men, without explaining how men could have initially created the conditions for such an appropriation, why women didn't resist it, or why it should be assumed that the reproductive function was ascribed as a lower social value than productive ones from the very start of all historical trajectories. The point of arrival (the lower value attached to functions carried out by women) is seen in these arguments as a *natural* basis, a given which merely reinforces the very notions they are supposed to combat.

In Lacanian quarters, gender is considered an expression of the psychic human need to classify the world symbolically in order to better organize and conceptualize it. Thus, following Lévi-Strauss's reasoning, Lacanian authors see gender as inscribed in the very symbolic patterning of language. Again, this fails to explain why language should have been configured in this particular way and not in any other that did not imply inequality (cf. Butler 2004: 43). Lévi-Strauss himself had proposed the incest taboo as one of the foundations of society, which, in his view, turned exogamy and the exchange of women—and therefore their objectification by men—into a constituent part of all social orders. Although it has been some years since Roy Wagner (1972) proved this argument to be untenable, and despite subsequent criticisms (Rubin 1975; Amorós 2009), this view continues to gather support to this day.

Equally problematic in considering *natural* every historical starting point based on inequality—and therefore giving up any attempt to explain it—the most brilliant representatives of contemporary structuralist anthropology (Descola 2001; Viveiros de Castro 2001; Vilaça 2002; Taylor 2001) have, over the past few years, defended the convenience of ignoring the concept of gender altogether. These authors consider that gender should be subsumed into two wider and more significant categories of social organization: female gender traits would be a function of the characteristics that define consanguinity (bonds cultivated with relatives and people within our own social circle), while male gender traits would define relations of affinity (links kept with strangers). In these authors' view, the fact that in most known societies women seem to be in charge of the former, while men look after the latter, would have determined female subordination. This is so because affinity is hierarchically superior and constitutes the "given dimension of the cosmic relational matrix," whereas the scope of consanguinity is limited to human relationships (Viveiros de Castro 2001: 19 and 26). In fact, Viveiros de Castro affirms that consanguinity can be seen essentially as the absence of affinity, renovating the well-established and resonating definition of the feminine as the *absence* of the masculine. Although it would appear that women's reproductive function is at the basis of this association, these authors do not explicitly state why they think this should cause men and women to specialize in these different types of relationships, and in any case, they fail to explain why these relationships should be read hierarchically and not in complementary or egalitarian terms (cf. Hernando 2010).

As presented above, all of these arguments seem to share the assumption that men's domination (in the case of materialists) or the prevalence of the masculine (in the case of Lacanians and structuralists) is *natural* and that it neither has an origin nor requires further explanation, for it is seen as inherent to the very constitution of society. Throughout this book, I shall defend a very different approach to this question as, in my opinion, the concept of *gender* refers to nothing but *differences in men's and women's respective degrees of individuation*. As we shall see, departing from an identity I call *relational* (non-individuated) and which is typical of both sexes in hunter-gatherer societies, our group's historical trajectory has gradually become defined by an increase in men's individuating traits, whereas, until late modernity, women maintained the same relational identity which had so far been shared by all group members. Men's and women's varying degrees of individuation reached a maximum difference (and became more widespread than ever before) at the time John Money carried out his study (the mid-1950s in US society). Throughout the entire previous historical process, however, it had been less acute the less socio-economically complex society had been. This means that the concept of *gender* refers to different degrees of difference between men's and women's identities, although, from a certain point in history, this difference came to imply a power relation in all cases. I write "a certain point in history" because I don't believe that sexual relations had always entailed power relations, which makes me question whether it makes sense to use the term *gender* in societies where power did not (or does not) define any social relation, that is, in the societies that Fried (1967) dubbed as "egalitarian societies." This historical process must have been one of such a subtle and gradual increase in men's traits of individuation/power that women themselves might have participated without noticing the subordination this would eventually bring about. And once it actually took place, the relationship was irreversible. This means that I do not consider the subordination of women to be universal but the result of a historical process which should be explained in cultural terms and not as the *natural* product of women's reproductive function (however much that function can be its condition and its point of departure).

First, let us examine our origins as a species in order to understand our biological foundations. Then we shall analyze the construction of identity in societies without any division of functions—except for the one resulting from the complementarity of the sexes—or work specialization, so as to enable a more profound analysis of such a problematic point of departure.

References

Amorós, C. (2009). *Vetas de Ilustración*. Madrid: Cátedra.
Burin, M. (1996). Género y psicoanálisis: Subjetividades femeninas vulnerables. In M. Burin & E. D. Bleichmar (Comps.), *Género, psicoanálisis, subjetividad* (pp. 61–99). Buenos Aires: Paidós.
Butler, J. (2004). *Undoing gender*. London: Routledge.
Cobo, R. (2005). El género en las Ciencias Sociales. *Cuadernos de Trabajo Social, 18*, 249–258.

Descola, P. (2001). The genres of gender: Local models and global paradigms in the comparison of Amazonia and Melanesia. In T. Gregor & D. Tuzin (Eds.), *Gender in Amazonia and Melanesia* (pp. 91–114). Berkeley: University of California Press.
Dio Bleichmar, E. (1998). *La sexualidad femenina. De la niña a la mujer*. Buenos Aires: Paidós.
Engelstad, E. (2007). Much more than gender. *Journal of Archaeological Method and Theory, 14*, 217–234.
Fried, M. H. (1967). *The evolution of political society*. Nueva York: Random House.
Gilchrist, R. (1999). *Gender and material culture: Contesting the past*. Nueva York: Routledge.
Haraway, D. (1991). *Simians, cyborgs, and women: The reinvention of nature*. Londres: Free Association Books.
Herdt, G. H. (1994). *Third sex, third gender: Beyond sexual dimorphism in culture and history*. Nueva York: Zone Books.
Hernando, A. (2010). Gender, individualization, and affine/consanguineal relationship. In L. H. Dommasness, T. Hjorungdal, S. Montón-Subías, M. Sánchez Romero, & N. L. Wicker (Eds.), *Situating gender in European archaeologies* (pp. 283–306). Budapest: Archaeolingua.
Jónasdóttir, A. G. (1994). *Love power and political interests. Towards a theory of pathriarchy in contemporary western societies*. Philadelphia: Temple University Press.
Molina Petit, C. (2000). Debates sobre el género. In C. Amorós (Ed.), *Feminismo y filosofía* (pp. 255–284). Madrid: Síntesis.
Money, J. (1965). Psychosexual differentiation. In J. Money (Ed.), *Sex research: New developments* (pp. 3–23). Nueva York: Holt, Rinehart and Winston.
Nicholson, L. (1990). Feminismo y Marx: Integración de parentesco y economía. In S. Benhabib & D. Cornell (Eds.), *Teoría feminista y teoría crítica* (pp. 29–48). Valencia: Edicions Alfons el Magnànim, Institució Valenciana d'Estudis i Investigació.
Posada Kubissa, L. (2007a). La diferencia sexual como diferencia esencial: Sobre Luce Irigaray. In C. Amorós & A. de Miguel (Eds.), *Teoría feminista: de la Ilustración a la globalización, Vol. 2: Del feminismo liberal a la posmodernidad* (pp. 253–288). Madrid: Minerva Ediciones.
Posada Kubissa, L. (2007b). El pensamiento de la diferencia sexual: el feminismo italiano. Luisa Muraro y 'El orden simbólico de la madre'. In C. Amorós & A. de Miguel (Eds.), *Teoría feminista: de la Ilustración a la globalización, Vol. 2: Del feminismo liberal a la posmodernidad* (pp. 289–317). Madrid: Minerva Ediciones.
Roca, I. M. (2005). La gramática y la biología en el género del español (1ª parte). *Revista Española de Lingüística, 35*(1), 17–44.
Rubin, G. (1975). The traffic on women. Notes on the political economy of sex. In R. R. Reiter (Ed.), *Toward and anthropology of women* (pp. 157–210). New York: Monthly Review Press.
Sanahuja, M. E. (2002). *Cuerpos sexuados, objetos y prehistoria*. Madrid: Cátedra.
Scott, J. (1986). Gender: A useful category of historical analysis. *American Historical Review, 91*, 1053–1075.
Taylor, A.-C. (2001). Wives, pets, and affines. In L. M. Rival & N. L. Whitehead (Eds.), *Beyond the visible and the material. The amerindianization of society in the work of Peter Rivière* (pp. 45–56). Oxford: Oxford University Press.
Vilaça, A. (2002). Making kin out of Others in Amazonia. *Journal of the Royal Anthropological Institute, 8*(2), 347–365.
Viveiros de Castro, E. (2001). GUT feelings about Amazonia: Potential affinity and the construction of sociality. In L. M. Rival & N. L. Whitehead (Eds.), *Beyond the visible and the material. The amerindianization of society in the work of Peter Rivière* (pp. 19–43). Oxford: Oxford University Press.
Wagner, R. (1972). Incest and identity: A critique and theory on the subject of exogamy and incest prohibition. *Man (New Series), 7*(4), 601–613.

Chapter 3
The Origin

Until the 1960s, the origins of human behavior had been explained mostly—and in the best of cases—by projecting onto the past the traits of contemporary hunter-gatherer societies. The resulting accounts overlooked fundamental behavioral differences between modern humanity and other human species prior to the appearance of *Homo sapiens* the hunter (such as *Homo habilis*, *Homo rudolfensis*, *Homo ergaster*, *Homo erectus*, Neanderthal, etc.) as well as nonhuman species as *Australopithecus*. The 1960s, however, saw Cambridge-trained Kenyan anthropologist, paleontologist, and archaeologist Louis Leakey (Johanson and Edey 1981: 83–84) establish a new approach to early human behavior: Leakey proposed that attempts to understand our own evolutionary origins should refrain from projecting the ways of their end product (contemporary hunters) onto the past and turn instead to the foundations of the original starting point. To this end, Leakey set out to supervise several doctoral theses about the behavior of modern-day representatives of the *hominid family* (the study of orangutans was taken up by Birutè Galdikas; gorillas were studied by Dian Fossey and chimpanzees by Jane Goodall), which were to completely transform our contemporary understanding and image of our earliest evolutionary steps. As we all know, the chimpanzee (genus *Pan*) is, in genetic terms, the most similar hominoid to our own species (Kehrer-Sawatzki and Cooper 2007) and so the *Pan troglodytes* (the only species of *Pan* known at the time) became the blueprint for most analogies with our own original behavior.

Insofar as they contribute to establishing a biological and evolutionary starting point for the construction of culture, the conclusions of research into hominid behavior are enormously valuable for an assessment of the pathways taken by human societies. These implications explain the importance of any statement about chimpanzee behavior and the scale of the conflicting interests and biases involved in this type of research.[1]

---

[1] Sarah Blaffer Hrdy (1999) documented the preferential attention traditionally payed by primatology to male over female behavior, drawing partial and even altogether incorrect conclusions. Donna Haraway (1989), in turn, devoted a book to portraying, among others, the biases generated by the influence of the Western world's own sociopolitical context (and such events as the world wars), on the changing emphasis of research on more aggressive or more cooperative aspects of chimpanzee behavior.

Until the 1980s, the only well-studied type of chimpanzee was *Pan troglodytes* or common chimpanzee, the object of Jane Goodall's in-depth doctoral thesis. Her groundbreaking research at Gombe (Tanzania) continues to provide relevant information to this very day and has shown, for example, that common chimpanzees can eat meat and use (but not produce) tools, that they live in parties dominated by males, that these are prepared to assert their territoriality in sometimes lethal confrontations with males from other communities, and that, at the beginning of their puberty, females leave their natal communities to join nearby parties. The sexual behavior of chimpanzees can be described as "casual promiscuity," where females from neighboring groups are selected by males under the strict imperatives of mating periods (Stanford 1998: 400–401). Over the years, Goodall has proven the existence of truly warlike gang rivalry, documented cases of cannibalism,[2] and recorded not-so-infrequent slaughter to consume the flesh of monkeys from several other species.

Therefore, the common chimpanzee, the only model available at the time to think about the original sociobiological organization from which our species had emerged, provided patriarchy with a *natural* basis.[3] These studies reinforced a narrative where women (the female representatives of the species) would have begun to free themselves of their initial state of domination after the Enlightenment through the development of reason. Inscribed by these studies in nature, domination could therefore be considered perfectly legitimate from a social point of view. These underlying ideas explain the scale of the interests and efforts invested in obscuring and discrediting research into a second type of chimpanzee that only became well known later, in the 1980s and 1990s, a species in which there is no domination of males over females, and thus provided an alternative model for the interpretation of our origins. This species is the *Pan paniscus*, also known as the pygmy chimpanzee, the dwarf chimpanzee, or the bonobo. In order to fully understand the implications of its appearance, we need to frame the discussion it affected so significantly in some detail.

---

[2] Hrdy (1999, Ch. 5) reviews the slaughterous and cannibalistic conduct of males of different primate species, including chimpanzees, against youths. Although this behavior was initially considered deviant, it is now recognized as widespread.

[3] Hrdy (1999) proposed a more complex hypothesis (along sociobiological lines), nonetheless stating that the domination over women stemmed directly from traces present in such primates as the common chimpanzee. In her opinion (ibid.: 187), female primates would have developed several strategies throughout their evolutionary history to cause uncertainty among males and reap the ensuing benefits for the survival of their offspring. Among them would have been "sexual receptivity beyond estrus, hiding ovulation, and assertive sexuality." In this way, at the historical moment when human groups began to guarantee paternal filiation, men—and their families—would have had to control women's sexuality, developing "cultural practices that reinforced the subordination of women and which enabled male authority over them." Presumably, women would have "adapted" to these forms of coercion by "becoming, among other things, more discreet and submissive."

3.1 The Origin of Humanity and Primate Behavior Patterns

Until 1974, studies about the origins of humanity had depicted the process of hominization as a gradual transformation of the traits of our predecessors in the evolutionary process. Bipedalism, encephalization—the growth of brain-to-body mass ratio which I shall refer to as the *growth of intelligence*—and the ability to make tools were assumed to have appeared as a single set of features. They were all thought to have developed as part of a single evolutionary process triggered by the reactivation of the Great Rift fault in East Africa. These assumptions were disproved in 1974, when it was discovered[4] that the three traits had not appeared simultaneously. Instead, it was established that bipedalism had appeared first, some 7 or 6 million years ago (Ma) with the emergence of the first primates which differed from chimpanzees only in their upright stance. And 4 million years later—that is, at 2.5 Ma—had bipedalism been coupled with an increase in intelligence and the production of tools. This second evolutionary step signaled the appearance of *Homo*, the genus that gradually came to develop the necessary cranial (and intellectual) capacity to enable the species *Homo sapiens* (at around 50,000 BC) to use symbols and complex culture.

These discoveries forced interpreters of the behavior of our evolutionary ancestors to distinguish two separate stages in the appearance of their traits: first, a hominid stage of unintelligent bipeds (such as *Australopithecus*), between 6 Ma and 2.5 Ma, and a second *Homo* stage of intelligent and toolmaking biped primates, whose appearance of 2.5 Ma marked the start of prehistory.

An interpretation of the first stage of early-hominid behavior was put forth by Manuel Domínguez Rodrigo (1994, 1997: 116–132), who proposed the "model of the social contract." Domínguez Rodrigo's approach conceptualized the behavior of these early hominids as a combination of the traits of two other primate groups: (common) chimpanzees, the closest to us in evolutionary terms, and cercopithecines—especially baboons. The latter are the only primates to have managed to survive in the savannah, in conditions similar to those faced by the earliest bipeds. As is now well known, thanks to Goodall, the opener the ecosystem chimpanzees are forced to live in, the more eclectic their diet becomes and the more cooperatively they behave to confront the greater threat of predators. But however diligently these primates try to organize, they cannot possibly survive in such an open environment and one so fraught with dangers as the savannah. Papio baboons have only been able

---

[4]This is the accepted year of the discovery of Lucy (a female *Australopithecus afarensis*) by Donald Johanson in Ethiopia. Lucy was perfectly bipedal but couldn't make tools as she was about as intelligent as a chimpanzee (between 400 and 450 cc). That time also saw the development of Charles Brain's studies of the South African caves where the first remains of *Australopithecus* had been discovered. Brain proved that, against the assumptions of their initial finder Raymond Dart, these beings had not been aggressive hunters but the almost defenseless victims of deadly savannah predators. This meant that, in its earliest evolutionary stage, hominization had not been associated to either meat consumption, making tools, hunting, or intelligence Cf. Johanson and Edey (1981).

to survive in these conditions by adopting a social pattern described as *oligarchic-hierarchic*—i.e., a male-dominated structure where the greatest-sized member or the alpha male of the group successfully confronts the fierce predators of the savannah in open fights. Domínguez Rodrigo suggested imagining the behavior of those unintelligent early hominids as a synthesis of the behavior displayed by the more eclectic and cooperative chimpanzees and that of dominant-male-structured cercopithecines. If this had been the case, the behavior of *Australopithecus* could be imagined as an amalgamation of chimpanzee and baboon behavior, although in contrast to the latter's formidable fangs—of great defensive and intimidating value—*Australopithecus* would have turned to the possibility, afforded by bipedalism, of using sticks and stones to threaten predators. To confirm this hypothesis, it would have to be proven, first, that male *Australopithecus* were—like male baboons—considerably bigger than females, suggesting the existence of dominant males. Secondly, that the grouping patterns of *Australopithecus* are similar to those of chimpanzees, whose social organization corresponds to joint free-roaming groups (Domínguez Rodrigo 2004: 69). Time has proven this theory right, as several paleontological and archaeological findings have confirmed both points.[5] It would therefore appear that this first hominization stage of unintelligent bipeds could be characterized by the existence of a male-dominated group pattern, one which, as Domínguez Rodrigo had anticipated, combined chimpanzee cooperation with the oligarchic group dynamics of *Papio* baboons.

The question is: can this same model be applied to the second stage that, from 2.5 million years onwards, brought about an increase in these already biped beings' intelligence and their ability to use tools? This fascinating question does not seem to have aroused much interest on the part of researchers. Instead, most continue to apply to this second stage the same model which, having proven successful for the first stage, endorses the natural and biological legitimation of male domination at the origin of our species. And yet a large body of research allows us to differ. Before we turn to this, let us examine the exact meaning of the appearance of *Homo* more closely since this evolutionary event did not come about as a gradual development of preexisting features but as a radical break off from the biological and behavioral traits which had so far defined primates.

The defining features of what we refer to as *Homo* appeared as a result of a genetic change called "Neoteny B." This change took place in West Africa some 2.5 Ma and involved an elongation of the growth stages of the infant members of some of these (already biped) groups, by which their fetal, infantile, and youth stages became more prolonged (Bermúdez de Castro and Domínguez Rodrigo 1992; Thompson et al. 2003). The change is easily understood if we compare the

---

[5] The first was confirmed by the finding of the famous footprints of *Australopithecus afarensis* in Laetoli (Tanzania) and the discovery of the male specimen AL-444-2 in Hadar, of a size significantly greater than Lucy's or that of any other female (cf. Kimbel et al. 1994). The second point was confirmed by the discovery of the so-called First Family, also found by Johanson in Hadar in 1975, and consisting of 13 individuals—among them 5 children—who died at the same time (Johanson and Edey 1981: 208–219).

3.1 The Origin of Humanity and Primate Behavior Patterns

development pace of the common chimpanzee with that of *Homo sapiens*: while a chimpanzee's infantile stage reaches into their fourth year of age and their youth lasts until the age of 11 or 12, humans are infants until the age of 10–12 and young until they reach 18–20 (Domínguez Rodrigo 1996: 157). This prolongation is also noticeable in the duration of the fetal stage, a period when primates' brains become half the size they will eventually reach in their adult stage. In all other primates, this cycle of growth is completed inside the mother's uterus. For example, a chimpanzee is born with a brain capacity of about 200 cubic centimeters—the maximum size they will ever reach being 450 cubic centimeters (ibid.). However, our own species' brains are so big (around 1350 cubic centimeters) that if we were born at the end of fetal life, that is, once our brain had reached half of that volume—about 700 cubic centimeters—we could not possibly fit through a birth canal compatible with bipedalism (we must bear in mind that 700 cubic centimeters is the brain size of a 1-year-old baby, that is, an infant with a 21-month gestation life). Nature seems to have found an adaptive solution, an exception to the norm for all other primates (including those which had spearheaded the first stage, such as *Australopithecus*) (ibid.: 158): unlike all other primates' infants, ours are born with just one third of the cranial size they will eventually acquire in their adult stage, an average of 380 cubic centimeters. This volume is reached in the ninth month of pregnancy, so, after birth, the first 12 months of extrauterine life are devoted basically and essentially to completing that growth. Our species' fetal life, *Homo sapiens*, lasts 21 months, the time required for the cranium to reach half of its adult size. Only 9 of these 21 months can be spent inside the womb, in order for babies' heads to fit through their mothers' birth canal (ibid.; see also Arsuaga 2001: 225–226). This fact had already been recorded in 1941 by Adolf Portmann, who noted that "the growth of the brain occurs during the twelve months following labor at the same accelerated pace as inside the uterus, and only after a year of extrauterine life does the pace of brain growth decrease (in relation to the body's)" (Arsuaga 2001: 225). Although the first *Homo* specimens had a lower average brain capacity than was later attained by *sapiens*, the information available suggests that all representatives of the *Homo* genus would have characteristically spent part of their gestation period outside of the uterus, and it was the consequences of this very fact that defined their behavior. As a result, our genus not only has the most intelligent infants in the animal kingdom—as their brains grow for much longer—but also the frailest and most dependent. Being so premature, the first year of their life is a remarkably fragile and passive one, not too different from the time spent inside the uterus (Domínguez Rodrigo 1997: 77–78). This must have required a complete transformation of the dynamics of cooperation in order to ensure their survival.

The genetic change in Neoteny B that brought about such fundamental changes took place at a time of climate change in East Africa. Palynological and paleontological data have dated the onset of this change at some 2.8 Ma and the ensuing and conspicuous drying up of savannah landscapes at around 2.5 Ma, at the exact same time of the genetic changes that signaled the appearance of *Homo* (Arsuaga 2001: 285–286). As a result of this, scarce food resources were added to the greater fragility of *Homo*'s infants, making it highly likely that a complete restructuring of social relations was required and that survival was achieved through a significant increase in cooperation between males and females.[6] This increase in cooperation would also have enabled members of this species to exchange information more quickly, as their elongated infant stage and cranial capacity would have increased their ability to learn. All of these changes are encapsulated by the appearance of the first tools and archaeological sites, which signal the start of prehistory, at around 2.5 Ma.

Therefore, compelled by biological imperatives, the *Homo* genus would have displayed characteristically intense cooperative behavior among all group members to ensure the survival of tremendously helpless and fragile infants in the harsh conditions of the dry savannah. It is hard to imagine any other way in which they could have succeeded in feeding and protecting an offspring that requires the highest care and energy expenditure of all primates.

And yet pushing forward this delicate evolutionary process still required further changes: an increase in brain size such as the one caused by Neoteny B modifies the proportion of energy absorbed by different organs. Due to its sophisticated and delicate structure, the modern human brain uses up to one fifth of our body's total energy expenditure, so its growth must have meant an increase for *Homo* by comparison to the energy consumed by *Australopithecus*' brains. This increase could only be afforded at the expense of the energy consumed by other organs, so the herbivorous intestinal tract of *Australopithecus* was replaced with our own characteristically omnivorous tract (Aiello and Wheeler 1995). In turn, this required the consumption of meat—for its higher ratio of proteins per mass unit consumed—facilitated by tools, the making of which was made possible by the increased intelligence brought on by *Homo's* larger brain. Both of these anatomic and cultural strategies have been confirmed by the archaeological record at levels dated at around 2.5 Ma.[7] As a result of the transition from a (longer) herbivorous intestinal tract to a (shorter) omnivorous one, the thorax changed from a cone shape (characteristic of chimpanzees and *Australopithecus*) to a cylinder shape (Aiello and Wheeler 1995). This change coincided with another transformation, by which the size-based sexual dimorphism of the previous stage gave way to a sexual dimorphism of different body shapes. Indeed, it has been attested that from at least 1.5 Ma female hips' iliac crest elongated, causing their waists to have different shapes from those of males. Also, from this point on, male and female anatomies each present characteristic distributions of fat and muscles (Domínguez Rodrigo 2004: 31 and 101). The appearance of *Homo* is thus associated to the disappearance of size differences between males and females—which among chimpanzees and *Australopithecus* indicate the existence of dominant males—and to the appearance of a kind of

---

[6] Manuel Domínguez Rodrigo insists on this particularly relevant point, noting that the balance between cooperation and competition is a defining feature of the social organization of all primate species. See Hrdy (1999).

[7] The oldest human-made lithic instruments come from 2.5 to 2.6 Ma. levels at the site of Gona (Ethiopia) (Semaw et al. 1997). In turn, recent research carried out at the Olduvai Gorge (Tanzania) by Domínguez-Rodrigo has proven that hunting was also practiced from the Lower Paleolithic, at least since 1.8. Ma. (Domínguez Rodrigo et al. 2010; Bunn and Pickering 2010).

intersex cooperation which, while seemingly complementary, is difficult to describe in further detail.

Domínguez Rodrigo (ibid.: 31) argued that this change could have come about as the consequence of replacing a reproductive strategy based on pheromones—which dictate the intense and punctual attraction of estrus—with one based on a more permanent physical attraction, making it necessary to differentiate bodies. This brings us to human beings' lack of estrus, another difference between ourselves and chimpanzees which we still have to account for. Although Domínguez Rodrigo's explanation rests more on the biological foundations than on the complex set of transformations which generated our own species, a further step can be taken to trace the possible impact of these changes on the behavior and relationships between the sexes of our most remote *Homo* ancestors.

Until the 1980s, it had been thought that *Homo sapiens* was the only primate species without estrus,[8] a feature which set us apart from all other species and prevented the use of any alternative frameworks to those afforded by the common chimpanzee. However, from the mid-1980s, several researchers, including Frans B. de Waal (of the Living Links Center and Psychology Department, Emory University, Atlanta) and Takayoshi Kano (of the Primate Research Institute, Kyoto University, Inugama, Japan), began to publish information about another previously almost unknown chimpanzee species: *Pan paniscus*, also known as the dwarf or pygmy chimpanzee—despite being the same size as the common chimpanzee—or the bonobo.

Bonobos have mainly been studied at two reserves in Central Congo: Lomako and Wamba. Stanford (1998) provides a good synthesis of their defining features, which I now turn to summarize. But first, I must underline that the data provided by research on bonobos is so controversial for the legitimation of the patriarchal order that this information tends to be minimized, or even outright concealed, attesting to the power dynamics that always permeate the scientifically recognized *truth*. Just like the common chimpanzee, bonobos constitute polygamous societies of fusion and fission, with females leaving the group on reaching puberty to join neighboring communities. But, unlike common chimpanzees, female bonobos do not immediately become eligible partners for the dominant male of their new group. Instead, newly arrived bonobo females set up links with the females in their host groups. These bonds with the females are cultivated on an individual basis and often lead to newcomers eventually occupying the position of *alpha individual* or group leader. According to Stanford, "it is probably not true that males are not affiliative with each other; rather, their bonds may be less apparent, and perhaps less strong than female-female and female-male bonds tend to be" (ibid.: 404). However, the most surprising aspect of bonobo society is that these links established by newly arrived females in their host group are cemented by, among other mechanisms, sexual relationships. Bonobo females, like those of *sapiens*, are sexually receptive and active throughout the year and not only during their fertile periods (chimpanzee's estrus).[9]

---

[8] This information sustained Fisher's (1982) arguments.

[9] Before bonobos were well-studied, Hrdy (1999: Chap. 8) proved that, in order to increase their

In fact, sex is the main vehicle of their social relations, and they practice it constantly, with or without reasons, either because they are feeling cheerful or sad, when they are feeling nervous or relaxed, to break tensions or to reaffirm friendships, to avoid conflicts, etc. Bonobo sexuality is clearly not only geared toward reproduction but also, and fundamentally, toward intragroup communication. This is confirmed by an even more surprising feature—sexual relationships among bonobos are not just heterosexual but also homosexual (through genital rubbing in both sexes) and include an entire repertoire that had so far been thought of as exclusively human: masturbation, fellatios, *cunnilingus*, and frontal copulation (see also Domínguez Rodrigo 2004: 29). At the same time, "lethal intercommunity aggression, forced copulation and infanticide have never been observed" (De Waal, in Stanford 1998: 407), and hunting and meat consumption, increasingly documented among chimpanzees, are barely practiced by bonobos; for short periods of time, females allow infant carrying and care on the part of adult males, who exhibit these conducts explicitly. Neither of these conducts—mothers' acquiescence or male exhibitions of infant care and carrying—has ever been documented in common chimpanzee communities.[10] Finally, and unsurprisingly, while common chimpanzees present high levels of sexual dimorphism due to the existence of dominant males, size differences between male and female bonobos are much smaller, indicating the absence of hierarchy between the sexes. Bonobo communities are highly cooperative societies that use sex to establish relationships which are not only reproductive and where females take on dominant positions at least as much as males—and, judging by some fieldwork, to an even greater extent.

Although certain fundamental differences between human and bonobo sexuality have been rightly highlighted (Domínguez Rodrigo 2004: 22 and 29), it should not be overlooked that, not being dictated by hormonal cycles, neither species' sexuality is geared exclusively toward reproduction. In both cases, sexuality has an added function which is absent from other species: it is a means of relationship building and communication. It is therefore relevant to point out that in both species, this trait appears connected to another two features: the lack of sexual dimorphism in terms of significant differences in body size between males and females (which means no biological dominance of dominant males) and the highest level of intragroup cooperation. We might ask ourselves: is this not a sufficient reason to believe that the behavior of our most remote *Homo* ancestors could be more similar to that of the bonobo chimpanzee than to that of the common chimpanzee so insistently used as a reference for the *Australopithecus* of the first stage? Since the answer is obviously

---

offspring's chances of survival, females of many other primate species also have sexual relationships outside estrus, don't show any visible signs of ovulation, and display sexually assertive conducts (see Chap. 2 note 6). She also provided evidence of sexual relationships between females in other primate species. What is particularly striking about bonobos is that all of these traits constitute their behavioral norm. As opposed to other species, these traits don't appear in an isolated way but are part of their permanent behavior all year round.

[10] In Hrdy's opinion (1999: 91), "in no species is infanticide a common event," but "for many primates it is, and has been throughout [...] their evolutionary history, a recurrent hazard." Hence, the surprise this aspect of bonobo behavior has been met with.

affirmative, we might begin to ask ourselves about the reasons why, despite all the information available, the common chimpanzee, with its male-dominated societies, continues to be used as the model analogue for the earliest stages of our *Homo* development, effectively blocking the bonobo from being brought forth to assess the validity of these analogies. De Waal (quoted in Stanford 1998: 407) has pointed out two major deliberate strategies in obscuring the importance of bonobos for human evolution and favoring common chimpanzees to emphasize war, hunting, tool use, and male domination: the first consists in portraying bonobos as an anomaly, allowing researchers to ignore them; the second strategy is to minimize the differences between both species of *Pan*, overstating their similarities and undermining the specific model value of bonobos. In both cases, the importance of bonobos for an understanding of the origin of human societies is masked. This comes as no surprise if we consider that acceptance of evolutionary ancestors with bonobo-like behavior could undercut the seemingly *natural* character of the patriarchal order and might threaten the alleged norm of heterosexuality. It would certainly put an end to the claim that the roots of the subordination of women lie in our animal or biological nature. Other grounds would be required to explain this subordination, and those who continue to defend it (alongside heterosexuality) as society's *natural* order would be delegitimized.

Since *Homo* required an increase in intergroup cohesion and cooperation to guarantee the survival of their offspring, a sexuality which was not strictly reproductive is very likely to have contributed to these ends (Hrdy 1999), as much as a new and previously completely unknown tool, exclusive to our own species: language. Psychologist Robin Dunbar (1997) argues that language may have reinforced the effect of care and grooming—already present in chimpanzee relationships—on strengthening bonds. According to Dunbar, when a group's size exceeds a certain number of individuals, the possibility of individual physical contact between each member and all others is lost. Language, brought about by an increase in brain size as a result of the neotenic change, would have allowed group cohesion and the establishment of group communication and bonds in increased groups, such as *Homo*'s. In my opinion, sexuality should be granted a pivotal role in the transition from one relationship model to the other, suggesting a framework that can arrange primates into increasing levels of cooperation and communication. First, cooperative *grooming*-practicing species like the common chimpanzee, followed by even more cooperative chimpanzees (like bonobos), which also use sexuality as a tool of social cohesion, and finally even more intelligent and cooperative primates (*Homo*), having added language to both of these strategies, made a quantum leap forward from the previous species' levels of cooperation.

It has therefore been ascertained that the behavioral model of the first *Homo*—that is, the origin of our species—may be placed at a substantial distance from the picture of an aggressive and male-dominated primate community inspired by the example of the common chimpanzee. It seems altogether more plausible that this second major stage in the origin of humanity, defined by the intelligence enabled by neoteny, might have been pioneered by a highly cooperative society. One with faster and more effective information flows, and which, thanks to the development of language and group cohesion, among other factors, permitted the necessary skills for toolmaking to be taught and learned more easily, in turn granting easier access to the necessary meat for *Homo*'s brain. More prolonged early developmental stages would have brought about longer learning processes, further boosting the entire process. The image elicited by this society appears radically different from the male-dominated societies of *Australopithecus*, and the idea that bonobo's egalitarian society might provide a more adequate model for analogies with the early *Homo* society seems to be gaining momentum. But then, a further question emerges from all of this: if the patriarchal order was not written in stone by either biology or nature, how can we explain its ever-present appearance in all historical trajectories? To approach this question, we must turn to yet another obvious one: what are the differences between bonobos and *Homo sapiens*?

3.2 What Do We Humans Have that Bonobos Lack?

Two essential differences between *Pan paniscus* and *Homo sapiens* fall within the scope of this book:

(a) As explained above, unlike bonobos, we humans have children whose first year of extrauterine life is similar to the fetal life of other primate species. This trait—which makes them the most fragile and dependent infants of all primates—was presumably associated to a *reduction in the mobility* of early *Homo* females, a strategy likely to have been adopted as a way of reducing risks. In order to sustain this argument without my ascribing to females a responsibility which could have been taken up by males, two points should be borne in mind: (i) we need to refrain from projecting our contemporary concept of *father* onto the past—in *sapiens* hunter-gatherer societies, the bond between men and offspring tends to be indirect, as the scientific bases of conception are unknown in these contexts. Also, (ii) *Homo sapiens* infants depend on breast milk for at least the first year of their lives. In hunter-gatherer societies, this period tends to be longer, both due to the nutritional value of mother's milk and because—by diminishing fertility—lactation operates as a birth-control mechanism, which is a *sine qua non* condition for survival.

Also, it would have become necessary to consume meat in order to maintain our notably expanded brains, which enable the development of the hunting activities that bonobos do not carry out. These have been confirmed for *Homo sapiens* at least at 1.8 Ma., at the Lower-Paleolithic site of Olduvai (Tanzania). Given the fragility of infants and their dependence on lactation, it seems likely that the type of cooperation needed by groups to organize and survive could have consisted on a distribution of functions where the men would have presumably taken on those activities which implied greater risks and mobility.

I would like to highlight that I am not defending the existence of differences between the activities themselves but stressing the importance of the differences in the *mobility* they implied. In itself hunting does not necessarily imply a hierarchic relationship over looking after offspring, and we cannot lose sight of the fact that women also contribute to obtaining food on a regular basis. The only difference between their activities and the ones carried out by men is that women tend to entail less risks. In fact, empirical evidence from ethnographic fieldwork in nonindustrial societies illustrates a complementarity in the functions carried out by each sex, which would be distributed according to the risks they involve (Murdock 1967). In general, men tend to take on riskier activities (which also require greater mobility), regardless of what they actually are. This explains why there are no universally masculine or feminine tasks, except high-risk ones, such as whaling and metalsmithing, which are universally masculine, as is, almost without an exception, hunting great terrestrial mammals. Fieldwork shows that, in most nomadic hunter-gatherer groups, men are in charge of larger game, while women hunt smaller animals and/ or are in charge of gathering—although they can occasionally assist in or carry out the former (Hernando et al. 2011). Among groups that continue to hunt but where horticulture is present, this is practiced by women, and the men hunt. In nonhunting horticulturalist groups, the men are in charge of growing the crops, and the women look after the domestic space; among farmers, where intensified production requires all the workforce available, both sexes tend to work in the fields, but it is usually the men who carry out the trade and exchange tasks enabled by surplus production and so on and so forth. It could then be presumed that, as opposed to bonobos, early human societies may have presented differences in the *mobility* of male and female members. As I shall contend, this difference would have been the profound and structural root of a slight variation in their respective modes of identity, which eventually brought about what is known as the *gender norm* (Hernando 2000).

(b) It has been explained above that, unlike bonobos, *Homo* developed a communication and cohesion tool of incalculable proportions: language. Although there is some discussion about the limitations and nature of early *Homo* language, it seems that, to a certain extent, this capacity was present from the very start (Arsuaga and Martínez 1998: 311–314; Domínguez Rodrigo 1997: 191–196). Language as we know it today was only developed with the appearance of *Homo sapiens*, although where and when this happened exactly is still the subject of debate (Henn et al. 2011; Hurford et al. 1998). The fact is that around 50,000 BC, an expansion can be detected from Africa, pioneered by an increasingly dense human group (*Homo sapiens sapiens* or modern *sapiens*) that came to substitute all previously settled populations in the remaining continents. So far, it is unclear whether parallel development of *sapiens* may have also occurred simultaneously in the Far East—a debate we shall not enter—but modern *sapiens* undoubtedly owed their success to a far more versatile, operative, and effective culture, a culture which allowed them to adapt to any environment, face up to any circumstance, and overcome any obstacle whatsoever and which has never ceased to transform itself to this day. The main difference between this species and all the previous ones lays in their mentioned ability to manipulate symbols. This allowed modern *sapiens* to confer meaning to the material visible dimension, to create mythical worlds to house the dead and through which to dispel fears, and to imagine Gods that bestowed meaning upon the world and cared for and protected those who believed in them.

This revolutionary ability to endow the world with meaning must have transformed their experience of it completely. Through language, a certain dimension was entered which is common to all members of the *sapiens* species and which sets us transcendentally apart from all preexisting primates, whether bonobos or other representatives of *Homo*. We *sapiens* live in a symbolically construed world. We confer meaning and value to our own actions and to the world's dynamic phenomena. And also to the sexes. This capacity—which is altogether lacking in bonobos—would eventually allow us, at a very advanced point in the process, to allocate differential social value to each one of them, in what is commonly known as *gender identities*.

3.3 Recapitulation and Starting Point

The point of departure for *sapiens* humanity could thus be described as follows: constituting highly cooperative and cohesive groups, *sapiens* used both sex and language as means of communication and the latter to transmit information. These groups were not male dominated but defined instead by a basic functional complementarity between males and females. Males specialized in those tasks which required higher mobility and risks, such as hunting, and females took on the care of an increasingly dependent and fragile offspring. Neither of these activities is either structurally or necessarily associated with power, which does not operate in a differentiated and personalized way among contemporary hunter-gatherers, and must therefore have also been absent from past ones. Consequently, if the course of subsequent historical trajectories saw women's maternity become associated to subordinate positions, the underlying reasons should be accounted for, as this is not an intrinsic feature of these activities *per se*.

As well as this, around 50,000 BC *sapiens* began to use symbols, as attested by the appearance of Upper-Paleolithic rock art. This enabled *sapiens* groups to provide the world with an order and meaning that could mitigate the anguish its immeasurable complexity might otherwise have caused. The construction of that order is dictated by the parameters of time and space, as our minds can only conceive of phenomena in terms of those two dimensions, making them part of the reality we live in. Through these parameters, we arrange only those phenomena that we are equipped to control to a sufficient extent. For this reason, no human group lives in a reality they consider out of their control (Hernando 2002). As an ordering parameter, *space* sets fixed references to establish relationships between the disorderly phenomena of reality, providing them with an order that makes them conceivable, whereas the parameter *time* operates through dynamic, recurrently moving references (Elias 1992). Writing renders these references abstract, as is the case with

3.3 Recapitulation and Starting Point

maps, borders or the administrative boundaries of space, or the time intervals of clocks. But in societies where writing does not exist, such as oral societies, references are made to coincide with the very elements of nature that need to be ordered.[11] In this case, fixed elements such as trees, rocks, or rivers are used as landmarks to order the world in spatial terms—"this happened by the river," "beyond the great tree," and "around the bend." In turn, recurrently moving elements—such as the sun, the moon, and the tides—are used as time references. This means that oral societies can only order that part of nature which they know firsthand, walk through on a daily basis, or live in—as abundant ethnological information proves—because that part contains the necessary ordering references. Nothing can be ordered unless it has been witnessed personally, and only on these grounds can it become a part of the reality which is thought to be inhabited. In turn, the further and wider the territory is roamed, the more phenomena will be incorporated into that reality, rendering it more complex and diverse but also more threatening and hazardous. In this way, unless space is represented through writing, the greater a person's (or a human group's) mobility, the wider the world will become for them, and the greater resolution will be needed to confront it. This difference in the capacity for resolution will imply a slightly higher level of personal individuation shared by those persons with a greater mobility, which will in turn constitute the basis of what is known as *gender* (from the beginning, men must have been slightly more individuated than women). This explanation takes the causative value away from hunting or maternity *per se*. The relevance of these *specializations* lies exclusively in their implications on the mobility of the tasks undertaken by each part and not in any intrinsic value of specialization itself. For this reason, when maternity no longer imposes limitations on mobility—as is the case in modernity—it ceases to bring about power differences. In the early stages of the evolution of *sapiens*, *it was not maternity but the lesser mobility* of females by comparison to males' that would have caused this minor cognitive difference between them. This factor, which did not imply any power differences in principle, might have constituted the basis of certain dynamics, which through their constant reinforcement would have been boosted to the point that they eventually came to shape a social order based on the domination of men over women.

The complementarity of functions brought on by the need to bring up an extremely dependent offspring would have *normalized* heterosexuality, which, as the case of bonobos proves, has no natural basis whatsoever. Nature freed both species from the irresistible—yet far more reproductively efficient—constraints of an impelling estrus. Nature also prolonged the frame of sexual relationships throughout the stages of the hormonal cycle, whether the female was fertile or not. These changes must have occurred because some function of sexuality other than

---

[11] I have dealt with the topic of the perception of reality through the use of either metaphors or metonymies to represent time or space in Hernando (2002). In that book, I bring together the arguments put forth by Elias (1992) about ordering reality through time and space and those proposed by Olson (1994) about the implications of using metaphoric or metonymic signs to represent reality.

reproduction was as vital as generating an offspring. This function cannot possibly be any other than communication to increase group cooperation and boost social bonding, as is also documented by the case of bonobos.

Let us turn now to how identity is created among groups where there is no division of functions or labor specialization and to the type of information available about the relationships between men and women in those societies.

References

Aiello, L. C., & Wheeler, P. (1995). The expansive-tissue hypothesis: The brain and the digestive system in human and primate evolution. *Current Anthropology, 32*(2), 199–221.
Arsuaga, J. L. (2001). *El enigma de la esfinge*. Barcelona: Areté.
Arsuaga, J. L., & Martínez, I. (1998). *La especie elegida. La larga marcha de la evolución humana*. Madrid: Temas de Hoy.
Bunn, H. T., & Pickering, T. R. (2010). Bovid mortality profiles in paleoecological context falsify hypothesis of endurance running-hunting and passive scavenging by early Pleistocene hominins. *Quatery Research, 74*(3), 395–404.
Domínguez-Rodrigo, M. (1994). *El origen del comportamiento humano*. Madrid: Librería Tipo.
Domínguez-Rodrigo, M. (1996). *En el principio de la humanidad*. Madrid: Síntesis.
Domínguez-Rodrigo, M. (1997). *El primate excepcional. El origen de la conducta humana*. Barcelona: Ariel.
Domínguez-Rodrigo, M. (2004). *El origen de la atracción sexual humana*. Madrid: Akal.
Domínguez-Rodrigo, M., Bunn, M., Mabulla, H. T., Baquedano, E., & Pickering, T. R. (2010). Paleoecology and hominin behavior during Bed I at Olduvai George (Tanzania). *Quatery Research, 74*(3), 301–303.
Dunbar, R. (1997). *Grooming, gossip and the evolution of language*. Cambridge, MA: Harvard University Press.
Elias, N. (1992). *Time: An essay*. Oxford: Basil Blackwell.
Fisher, H. (1982). *The sex contract. The evolution of human behavior*. New York: W. Morrow.
Haraway, D. (1989). *Primate visions. Gender, race and nature in the world of modern science*. Routledge: Londres.
Henn, B. M., Gignoux, C. R., Jobin, M., Granka, J. M., Macpherson, J. M., Kidd, J. M., et al. (2011). Hunter-gatherer genomic diversity suggests a southern African origin for modern humans. *Proceedings of the National Academy of Science (PNAS), 108*(13), 5154–5162.
Hernando, A. (2000). Hombres del tiempo y mujeres del espacio. Individualidad, poder y relaciones de género. In: P. González Marcén (Coord.), *Espacios de género en arqueología* (Special Issue of Arqueología Espacial 22, pp. 23–44).
Hernando, A. (2002). *Arqueología de la Identidad*. Madrid: Akal.
Hernando, A., Politis, G., González Ruibal, A., & Coello, E. B. (2011). Gender, power and mobility among the Awá-Guajá (Maranhão, Brasil). *Journal of Anthropological Research, 67*(2), 189–211.
Hrdy, S. B. (1999). *The woman that never evolved*. Cambridge, MA: Harvard University Press.
Hurford, J. R., Studdert-Kennedy, M., & Knight, C. (Eds.). (1998). *Approaches to the evolution of language*. Cambridge: Cambridge University Press.
Johanson, D. C., & Edey, M. (1981). *Lucy. The beginning of humankind*. Nueva York: Simon and Schuster.
Kehrer-Sawatzki, H., & Cooper, D. N. (2007). Structural divergence between the human and chimpanzee genomes. *Human Genetics, 120*(6), 759–778.

References

Kimbel, W. H., Johanson, D. C., & Rak, Y. (1994). The first skull and other new discoveries of Australopithecus afarensis at Hadar, Etiopía. *Nature, 368*, 449–452.

Murdock, G. P. (1967). *Ethnographic atlas*. Pittsburgh: University of Pittsburgh Press.

Olson, D. R. (1994). *The world on paper. The conceptual and cognitive implication of writing and reading*. Cambridge: Cambridge University Press.

Semaw, S., Renne, P., Harris, J. W., Feibel, C. S., Bernor, R. L., Fessehay, N., & Mowbray, K. (1997). 2.5-million-year-old stone tools from Gona, Ethiopia. *Nature, 385*, 333–336.

Stanford, C. B. (1998). The social behavior of chimpanzees and bonobos. Empirical evidence and shifting assumptions. *Current Anthropology, 39*(4), 399–419.

Thompson, J., Gail, L., Krovitz, E., & Nelson, A. J. (2003). *Patterns of growth and development in the genus Homo*. Cambridge: Cambridge University Press.

Chapter 4
Relational Identity (or Identity When One Has No Power over the World)

4.1 Relational Identity

There is no such thing as a human group without any functional division or work specialization. All known cases present at least one fundamental division: certain functions are fulfilled by women and others by men. As discussed in the preceding chapters, this difference could be attributed to what appears to be the need to carry out these functions in a mutually complementary way, so that an extremely dependent and vulnerable offspring can be seen too. Still, there is no reason why this division should affect the value attached to each one of these sexually defined tasks.

Let us take as an example a group with the least imaginable degree of functional division (where some activities are distributed by sex), such as present-day hunter-gatherer groups living in small and highly mobile bands. Amazonian hunter-gatherer groups provide good examples of these, and I shall refer to them several times throughout this book, as ethnographic fieldwork has allowed me to study their dynamics in depth. These groups are called "egalitarian societies" (Fried 1967), because they have no chiefs or specialists of any kind. There is no writing among them either, so communication is exclusively oral: they rely on personal relationships to transmit knowledge and have not developed formal logic or the abstract classifications inherent to science (Ong 1982; Havelock 1986). Therefore, when it comes to explaining nonhuman natural dynamics, these groups attribute to them the only form of behavior they know, that is, human behavior, projecting social behavior onto the entire realm of existence, both human and nonhuman. These groups generally have a perfect understanding of the recurrences and associations of natural phenomena, and they only rarely need to ask themselves about the ultimate cause of these events. But if anything unexpected or irregular does take place, explanations are invariably sought (and found) in humanlike relationships and agencies (Campbell 1989: 76): a clap of thunder is seen as caused by animals having fallen out with each other, or by their copulating, or as the result of someone having broken the group's rules. And yet, since nonhuman nature is seen as much more powerful than the group—for it can provide food or take it away, grant life or bring death—it becomes sacred. This is not done in an institutionalized manner or by virtue of any god inhabiting the abstract world of ideas, as in our own culture. Instead, hunter-gatherer groups assume that since nature operates in the same way as their own group, but is far more powerful, it presides over their destinies. The Q'echí', for example, are a group of horticulturalists from Guatemala with whom I carried out an ethno-archaeological project. They believed in the deity Tzultzak'á. Tzul means mountain and Tzak'á means valley, but Tzultzak'á's full name does not translate as "the god of the mountains and valleys," but as "valleys and mountains with human behavior…" and (one might add) "with more power than our own social group."

This way of perceiving nonhuman nature is, on the one hand, highly gratifying, as it allows these groups to establish profound personal and emotional ties with these momentous natural elements; on the other hand, however, their relationship with them is defined by impotence. Unaware of the abstract causal mechanisms that guide natural phenomena, these groups are incapable of controlling their effects and always adopt an "object" position toward the wishes and desires they attribute to nature. Agency over the world's dynamics lies not in these people's own hands but in the sacred instance that the group's survival depends on.

It could be said that members of these groups have neither personal pathways nor separate functions other than those assigned to their sex. For this reason, they do not conceive themselves as individually different from each other—as indeed they are not— and no member of the group is seen as potentially threatening by the rest, for there are no differences between members' power, specialization, and technological control. At the same time, these groups' circumstances make them incapable of foreseeing and controlling the effects of nonhuman nature, which, therefore, *does* become a powerful source of threats and danger. As a result, these groups' self-perception operates through what I call *relational identity*. This consists in seeing oneself as a mere part of a greater unit—one's own group—to increase one's feeling of security and strength in the face of the completely uncontrollable forces of nature. This type of identity stems from these persons' inability to conceive of themselves beyond the closely knit fabric of relationships that they are part of. A fundamental nuance must be clarified here: *relational identity* does not only imply that the persons themselves give a great deal of importance to their relationships (as may be the case with individualized people) but that it is simply impossible for anyone to conceive of themselves outside of those relational bonds.

Leenhardt (1979)—a protestant preacher and French ethnologist sent to New Caledonia in the early twentieth century—put it perfectly when he referred to the Canaco people's notion of personhood. To them, each person can only be conceived as a crossroad of all the relationships they are part of: "I am my son's father, my nephew's uncle, my sister's brother…" It is impossible to find within them an inner core, a differentiated and isolated particular identity; what we would call "the self." Left on their own, deprived of their relations, a Canaco person feels "a lost character. I don't know who I am" (ibid.: 155). This type of identity is shared by all group members, both men and women in hunter-gatherer groups; their lack of technological control over the world is such that they can only feel safe by seeing themselves as part of a greater unit, i.e., the group they belong to, which comes to constitute the smallest conceivable identity unit. The level of anguish and disorientation that can be caused by losing their relationship with the group is sometimes even greater than could be inspired by death, as the Txukahamei (better known as the Kayapó) of the Brazilian Amazon shows: the famous Villas Bôas brothers, mid-twentieth-century *sertanistas*—explorers who spent many years working in close contact with Amazonian indigenous groups—were astonished to discover that, if Kayapó individuals quarreled and broke off from their groups, "five or ten years later the refugees usually return, often to be clubbed to death by their victorious enemies" (Cowell 1973: 159). As the Kayapó could have survived perfectly well by themselves in the jungle, the Villas Bôas brothers concluded that the reason for their return was that "many Indians would rather die than live outside their group" (*idem*).

My argument is that, at the start of all historical trajectories, this kind of *relational identity* was shared by both men and women in every single social group. But as men began to occupy specialized positions and to develop different functions—and therefore positions of power—this type of identity became increasingly identified only with women, so we now know it as *female gender identity* ("I am my husband's wife and the mother of my children"). Far from being grounded in women's bodies, this type of identity is closely connected with an absence of technological control and the inability to explain the world through scientific reason, in other words, with powerlessness (we shall return to this point).

Human groups which operate through *relational identity* express this ascription visually by unifying their appearance: all group members dress in the exact same way and use the same ornaments and distinctive elements (on their lips or ears, body paintings, etc.) that differentiate them as a group. Material culture expresses ascription, since—as described above—the former also construes the latter through mutual codetermination: *looking like* part of the group is a powerful way of construing belonging, a mechanism which always operates similarly, regardless of cultural context. Again, consider youth subcultures—punks, goths, rappers, etc.—and the fundamental role that a unified appearance plays in them.

To summarize the points made so far, we could say that the less functionally divided a human group is, the more likely its members will be to recognize their bonds and their need for the group. Their relationship with the world around them will also be more emotional, as the group will understand the world's recurrences but insist on attributing them to an external agency, a sacred subject toward whom they adopt an "object" position. But have I not just posited that the whole purpose of identity mechanisms is precisely to make people feel safe in the universe? How can these groups feel safe if they see themselves as subordinate to a power so momentous that it appears uncontrollable and beyond influence? The answer is simple: these groups interpret nonhuman nature, which they consider sacred, by projecting onto it the traces of their own social group and by establishing a similarity with it which they then read conversely: as they consider themselves the only group that behaves in the exact same way as the sacred instance, they conclude that they have been *chosen* by that sacred instance to receive the necessary knowledge for survival. In fact, if we translate these groups' self-designations—the names they give themselves (Awá, Nukak, Q'eqchí')—without an exception these always mean the *true* human beings, the *real* people; *the* people vs the rest—i.e., those who have not been chosen by the sacred instance and do not have the same level of humanity. The strength of myth as a mechanism of self-reassurance lies in the fact that it construes the sacred instance in the image and likeness of the group and then concludes that, since this particular group is the only one to behave in the exact same way as the sacred instance, its members are *the chosen ones*, keepers of a secret knowledge that will save them among all others, bearers of the key to survival. Of course, survival can only be guaranteed as long as the divinity's desires are satisfied and it is granted due subordination and recognition, and this is where rituals come in. In order to guarantee a reassuring effect on those who believe in them, myths have to be constantly reenacted through rituals.

At this point, I would like to clarify quite an important point: in our own cybernetic and postindustrial society, those who exert power tend to idealize rational and scientific thought, identifying myths with the false and superstitious knowledge of legends or fairy tales. This assessment is completely wrong. Myth is the knowledge of faith, which, unlike scientific knowledge,[1] does not rest upon reason but emotion. It is a truth so authentic for its believers that it stands beyond verification: there is no point in questioning a Catholic about the physical existence of Heaven or Hell, for example, as their beliefs are not based on the type of empirical evidence that science relies on but on absolute emotional conviction. This provides mythical knowledge with a much greater power and the capacity to reach far beyond a person's mere understanding of certain concrete phenomena and into their most profound and internal core. In fact, very little changes in someone's life happen when they substitute one scientific truth for another, whereas if someone stops believing in a myth, their whole life, and indeed its very meaning, will change completely. So powerful is the transformation in their way of understanding life, relationships, and the world itself. Believing in a myth always provides comfort and protection, as its basic tenet is that a certain sacred instance has chosen us and will protect us as long as we indulge its wishes.

As a discourse of origins, myth legitimizes the absence of change as a key to survival; it prescribes the eternal recurrence of a way of life transmitted by the sacred instance. Myth is the legitimizing discourse of societies that, because they lack high levels of technology, see change as a risk they are not prepared to take. The concept of *risk*, Giddens reminds us (1991: 111), can be found as early as the sixteenth century in the works of Machiavelli, but it only became part of everyday Western language in the seventeenth century, along with uses of the word *individual* as a synonym for person. Only then, in the late Renaissance, did functional division and the control of technology enable most men to feel that their security depended more on the changes that they could cause themselves than on the endless repetition of a way of life handed down to them by their myth of origin (and, in the case of

---

[1] Mary Midgley (2004) has presented some very interesting arguments showing that the faith-like relationship we in the modern world have come to establish with science, places it in the category of myth. We shall return to this in Chap. 8.

4.1 Relational Identity

Europe, written in the Bible). As a result, growing numbers of these men (stimulated by the growth of socioeconomic complexity and the consolidation of their positions of power and specialization) began to value change as a key to survival rather than perceive it as a threat. It was the beginning of a transition which, by the nineteenth century, had seen myth give way to history as a legitimizing discourse of origins.

It was then that traditional positivist history began to acquire the same functions which had so far been fulfilled by myth, as well as inheriting some of its logical traps. Just as groups use myth to construct the sacred instance in their own image and likeness—to conclude that, given that very likeness, they have been *chosen* to survive—positivist history searches into the past for the very traits societies wish to legitimize in the present (in our case technology, power, individuality, reason), arriving at the conclusion that, since only these very traits can guarantee survival and no one has developed them quite like us, we are clearly the only ones who will survive (Hernando 2006).

Like myth, positivist history sees the past through the lens of its own social order, comforting society with a protective and soothing discourse. Both legitimizing discourses follow opposite but parallel paths: myth prioritizes the least dynamic parameter, *space*, as a way of denying the existence of change, and therefore reads the past in spatial terms, placing it in mythical places (such as Heaven and Hell), which are parallel to the present. History, on the other hand, prioritizes *time* and insists on organizing the past chronologically, to show that change is the key to our own *superiority* (our alleged greater level of *humanity*). Myth is based on a communitarian and relational concept of identity, while history espouses an individualized concept of identity.

As a narrative, the type of history construed by positivism and historicism is neither more complex nor more objective than myth. The main difference is that myth is brought into play when societies are faced with phenomena which cannot be explained by causative dynamics. In these situations, myths provide the kind of security that derives from continuity, as reassurance is gained from the thought that, in the present and known conditions, survival is granted. Security is guaranteed by permanence as in old adages (those remainders of premodern mentality) such as, "Better the devil you know than the devil you don't," that express the following reasoning: I know I have survived in the present conditions, so I assume I will continue to survive, but given my insecurity about the circumstances that surround me, I might not survive if these circumstances change. Myth legitimizes this fear of change, providing it with sacred standing: only eternal repetition of the very behavior transmitted by the divinity can guarantee survival.

In groups with no functional division of labor, impotence is therefore compensated by a great deal of emotional gratification, both because it fits in perfectly with relational identity and group bonds and because of its inextricable link to beliefs in a sacred instance which will protect and save if its wishes are granted. The fact that the group has been *chosen* by this sacred instance generates a feeling of protection and superiority over other human groups, though the condition of this choice is complete *subordination* to the sacred entity. It should also be borne in mind that the less control or scientific knowledge a group has over natural phenomena, the more it will project its own social order onto it, that is, the more it will make human beings the measure of all things, and the more self-referential its members' perceptions will become. This way, insecurity and impotence are compensated with the feeling that the group is the center of the universe (Eliade 1959; Ong 1982: 77). Only when a phenomenon is either understood through reason or controlled through technology (which are equivalent operations) it is perceived as being subject to its own dynamics, separate from human behavior. This means that as human beings become more confident in their own ability to survive, they can begin to recognize that the universe operates by rules that have little to do with themselves. The more secure we become, the greater our ability to recognize that we ourselves are not the center of the universe and that it exists apart from us (the same phenomenon takes on a personal scale, as I will analyze below). Remember, for example, the high price Copernicus had to pay for defending that it was not the Sun that rotated around the Earth but vice versa. Until a high level of security and confidence in one's own capacity to control the world is attained, the world is seen as spinning around oneself and construed by projecting the traits of one's own social group onto it.

On the other hand, the less socioeconomically complex a group is, the smaller the shifts in its everyday activities: day after day, its members will have the same routine, and the only conceivable changes will be associated to seasons or the varying resources obtained from the different territories they roam. Still, because this variation is cyclic, change is always marked by recurrence. Therefore, in these cultures, time always organizes repeated experiences and is not perceived as a linear arrow where the past was different from the present and the present is different from the future. As opposed to this, societies of little economic complexity conceive time as an eternal present or as a cycle that always goes back to its point of origin. The cycle only starts to open up very slowly as the range of everyday activities begin to broaden. Such cyclic perceptions reinforce a type of identity where each person can only conceive of themselves through this very recurrence, neutralizing the fear of change caused by a low level of technological development. A summary of this type of identity can be seen in Fig. 4.1.

However, if early in their histories human groups everywhere were characterized by *relational identity*—given their rudimentary technology and division of labor—is it then appropriate to use the term "gender" to describe the relationships between the sexes and the differences between them?

4.2 Gender in So-Called Egalitarian Societies

When the concept of gender was adopted by Money back in the 1950s, power differences between men and women were very probably at their historical peak. This difference had been increasing from the very beginning of all societies' historical trajectories, when growing numbers of men came to occupy differentiated and specialized social positions—i.e., as socioeconomic complexity and the internal division of society increased. For this reason, when the concept was taken up by the

4.2 Gender in So-Called Egalitarian Societies

Low levels of functional division and labor specialization
Recurrent activities
No awareness of the causal mechanisms of nonhuman nature, which is attributed human behavior. MYTH
Groups perceive themselves as the center of the universe
Emotional relationship (as well as non-abstract rational) with all the elements of reality
Nonhuman nature is perceived as threatening (as it is neither understood nor controlled)
Human nature is not perceived as threatening (all members have similar behavior)
RELATIONAL IDENTITY: Its core lies in the relationships established with others.
Change is negatively valued, because of the risks it implies Space constitutes the most visible axis of social organization.
FEELS POWERLESS BEFORE THE WORLD
Trust in destiny and survival is placed in a sacred instance, with whom a dependent and subordinate relationship is established
Security is based on the confidence of having been chosen by the sacred instance: OBJECT position
No desires are generated for oneself, and, instead, there is a permanent preoccupation to identify and satisfy those of the sacred instance who provides security

Fig. 4.1 Structural features of RELATIONAL IDENTITY

social sciences and feminism, power relations between the sexes came to be considered inherent to the very concept of gender (Scott 1986: 1067). The existence of these relationships is unquestionable in any society with differentiated positions of power because, as we shall see, it is upon that very domination that such power is built. But the concept requires some reflection when applied to societies where these relationships do not exist, such as egalitarian bands of hunter-gatherers.

This is not an easy question. Most researchers agree that all of these groups assign different functions to each sex in a mutually complementary way, but that this does not necessarily imply male domination (Sanday 1981; Rival 2007). In fact, having taken strictly economic factors or social hierarchy into consideration, researchers often conclude that these societies are *truly egalitarian* from the point of view of relations between the sexes[2] and therefore infer that the same must have been true in the early stages of their historical trajectories. However, when the subjectivities and symbolic aspects of bands are taken into consideration, men always have greater prestige or status,[3] even in those cases where women can enjoy a certain power (Ortner 1996: 141). According to these authors, we should not confuse *prestige* and *power*, and both ought to be considered in order to understand and value gender relationships in each situation (ibid.: 172). In order to better explain the difference between these two types of relationship, I will turn to the case of the Awá-Guajá of the Brazilian Amazon, among whom I did fieldwork with between 2005 and 2009[4] and whose relationship with the world is similar to other Amazonian groups (Hernando et al. 2011). The Awá call themselves Awá, though anthropologists call them Guajá to distinguish them from other Tupi-Guarani groups with the same self-denomination. Here, I will refer to them by the name they give themselves.

My work focused on the Juriti indigenous post, where employees of the FUNAI (the National Indian Foundation, under the Brazilian Ministry of Justice) try to grant them protection from the constant threat of their territories being ruthlessly invaded by illegal loggers (González Ruibal and Hernando 2010). Life inside reserves has forced the Awá to modify their traditional lifestyle in several ways, although some of its most important features can still be observed, and it is also possible to infer and distinguish other more recently transformed aspects. The most visible and important consequence of resettlement on reserves has been mobility restriction. Although the men in the group continue to hunt on a daily basis, the entire group no longer roams constantly like it used to. Instead, they spend the night next to the post, which complicates the task of obtaining the carbohydrates formerly attained by gathering, so FUNAI employees are teaching them to cultivate manioc. Traditional Brazilian peasant society considers agriculture a male activity, and therefore the employees are teaching the Awá men—who are also in charge of hunting—to grow crops, while the women—who used to be in charge of gathering—are left with almost nothing to do.

Americhá is the oldest woman in the group, her age calculated at about 90, and her restless roaming attests to the active participation once had by Awá women in group economy: she continues to gather, smoke, and dry fibers to make ropes for her

---

[2] See, for example, studies by Leacock (1992), Flanagan (1989), Lee (1982), Begler (1978), Kent (1993), Rival (2005, 2007), Zent (2006), etcetera.
[3] This is the point made by Ortner (1996), Rogers (1975) and Sanday (1981).
[4] R&D Project (Hum2006-06276), "Ethnoarchaeology of the Awá-Guajá, a group of hunter-gatherers in transition to agriculture (Maranhão, Brazil)", financed by the Spanish Ministry of Science and Technology.

4.2 Gender in So-Called Egalitarian Societies

skirt and hammock, to cut up immense leaves to renovate and expand her house, and to look for *michiraniká* (a kind of tree resin) for lighting, or she sets out on long excursions to find small animals in their burrows by herself and with a *machete*.... In contrast, young women barely carry out any activities at all, with gathering having been replaced with agriculture and turned into a male activity. The men, on the other hand, are overloaded with economic tasks: they now have to hunt, grow crops, clean, peel, and process manioc or rice, and do all the cooking—the ethnological literature describes how men and women used to cook what they each obtained (the men the meat they had hunted, the women, the vegetables they had gathered), which would explain why only the men cook now. These days, Awá men even wash the clothes that they have been given by the FUNAI rangers, imitating these men who spend long periods of time away from their families. Meanwhile, the women enjoy far easier days looking after babies, chatting or joining in on the occasional hunt. They assist male hunters by shouting and clapping to frighten monkeys on tree tops into stillness, or by running around after the monkeys on the ground, indicating which tree the hunters should climb next.

In spite of all these changes in the present economic contribution of men and women and the gender biases constantly being introduced by FUNAI personnel, the women in the group still retained an enormous power of decision—at least as much as the men, in what constitutes a clear remainder of gender relationships prior to their resettlement in the reservations. They participated in many important group decisions, including the relationships with our own research team: Ayrwoa, a particularly strong and authoritative woman would often decide, for example, whether or not we should be allowed to take part in hunts or whether food could be shared with us. Awá women would also often demand that their men go hunting to treat them to a certain type of meat or fish on a certain day, and the men tended to oblige without conflict or discussion.

On the other hand, while their first marriages are often arranged for them with an older man and regardless of their own preference, Awá women are thereafter free to split up and start new relationships as often as they wish. Furthermore, being unaware of the scientific foundations of human conception but able to connect it to semen, which is visible, but not to the—invisible—cycles of ovulation, they believe the fetus to need a constant supply of semen to renovate itself and to require that they have sexual intercourse with several male group members throughout pregnancy. These partners are chosen by the mothers and will later become the baby's multiple parents.[5] Relations often continue freely after pregnancy, as Awá women's relationships are not restricted to the man they consider their husband at any one time. The linguist in our research group, António Silva Santana—who demonstrated the very meaning of biblical "speaking in tongues" by astonishingly learning a

---

[5] Beckerman and Valentine (eds.) (2002) review the question of Amazonian *multiple paternity*. The specific case of the Awá is referred to by Forline (1997: 168) and Cormier (2003a: 64–65). From a sociobiological point of view, multiple paternity has been interpreted as an (unconscious) female strategy to ensure the involvement of several men in obtaining resources for their children's survival (Hrdy 1999: xxii).

Tupi-Guarani language in record time—can attest to the level of true harassment that Awá women are capable of. Their constant efforts to seduce António were encouraged by the amusement and support of all the men in the group—husbands included.

If this were the only level of behavior to be taken into consideration, it might correctly be concluded that Awá society is truly egalitarian, or that the power balance even tilts toward Awá women. But reality, of course, is far more complex and subtle. In fact, if we look closely at the symbolic level of this culture, we find that the masculine is constantly prioritized. To begin with, the very term "Awá" identifies the term "human" with "man," taking a part for the whole, as in our own culture. Accordingly, the Awá believe that only men can visit the mythical space inhabited by their dead, the heavenly *iwa*. If women wish to contact any of their ancestors, they are forced to send news through the mediating figure of a man. Women can take part in decorating men's bodies with feathers and can assist them in the increasingly high-pitched (and hyper-oxygenating) songs typical of this ritual. But it is Awá men who sing and perform the repetitive ritual dance as each one of them enters a leaf structure built to this end (*takaya*). There they remain for some time, then "fly away" from it, and finally return to it. The performance shows how women can only act as men's helpers, as assistants in their interactions with the mythical world, which is the ultimate source of legitimacy for the social order. Awá men's monopoly over this sacred instance is also expressed by biased interpretations of their dreams. Men's dreams are always seen as encounters with the *iwa*, the sacred instance, while women's dreams are considered episodes of possession by some deity or spirit (Cormier 2003b: 136). Men's roles in dreams are always very active, while the women are invariably ascribed passive roles, in yet another way of reinforcing perceptions of their respective functions in conception.

The Awá also seem to conform to what appears to be a norm in all Amazonian societies,[6] and one that structuralist anthropologists fail to explain, according to which the men take over relationships with strangers or affines whenever they entail risk, as is the case with the land-encroaching loggers—although this is not necessarily the case if the relationships are perceived as safe—as in Ayrwoa's interactions with our research team. Awá women specialize in looking after the group's children and—perhaps as a way of compensating and reacting to the loss of functions associated with gathering—expand their maternal functions to include breast-feeding of infant monkeys and other young animals, a common feature among many Amazonian groups (see, for example, Zent 2006: 13–14; Fausto 1999; Kozák et al. 1979). This process will very probably lead to their eventually adopting the gender distribution of functions typical of the peasant and modern Brazilian societies around them.

How, then, to assess the present situation? Is it possible to talk about "gender" when different functions do not entail palpable power inequalities on a day-to-day

---

[6] Some examples can be found in Viveiros de Castro (1992: 190–191), Fausto and Viveiros de Castro (1993), Gow (1989), Descola (2001), MacCallum (1990), Seymour-Smith (1991), Rival (2005), Silva (2001), Vilaça (2002), etc.

4.2 Gender in So-Called Egalitarian Societies

basis? Does the case of the Awá and other present-day hunter-gatherers help us understand the origins of inequality?

This point requires us to stop again and think about the validity of analogies between present-day indigenous peoples and past prehistoric groups, as, in most respects, comparisons can be highly problematic. Without a doubt, present-day hunters have a history which was lacking in prehistoric times. In fact, in many cases (including the Awá), their present situation is the result of historical trajectories which even included previous agricultural phases.[7] In this sense, no analogies can be made between past and present based on any one specific cultural trait, such as the content of their myths. However, analogies may have solid grounding—and it is my intention to establish them—if they compare structural relationships, that is, whenever it can be ascertained that a necessary relation holds between two terms. This means that if one of these terms exists in any one of two separate contexts, then the other term too must have necessarily existed in the other context (Gándara 1990). For example, if a human group presents no functional division of labor, writing, or transport technology, it can be inferred that maps will certainly be unknown to them and that the dimensions they ascribe to their universe will necessarily coincide with the boundaries of their lived space and their everyday knowledge of it. All extant ethnological literature proves this to be the case, so the idea that this must have been so in the early stages of all historical trajectories is the product of speculative reasoning, but also a solid analogy. For the same reason, if a group lacks technology and writing, it can be concluded quite safely that they will interpret reality through myths, even if the actual content of any one myth cannot be established or is irrelevant to the purpose of this book..., and so on and so forth. I intend to build my arguments based on this type of analogy, discarding other more contextual and historically bound cases.

Going back to the question of the historical origins of patriarchy, most proposals operate on the undeniable factual basis that the females of our species have to breast-feed an extremely dependent offspring; this could explain why, in all known cases, it should be the men who are in charge of the most dangerous tasks or of those requiring the highest mobility. The reasoning is also congruent with the fact that women specialize in relations of consanguinity while men focus on affinity, which in turn, also fits into arguments made by psychologists and psychoanalysts that, in the process of building their own personalities, young girls identify with their mothers—highlighting attachment and close links—while young boys need to separate and detach themselves from that same primary maternal figure (Chodorow 1978; Dio Bleichmar 1998; Levinton 2000). Without questioning the validity of these arguments—which must probably be taken into account—I consider that male domination over women does not necessarily follow from them automatically. It has been argued that the masculine sphere of action would have acquired greater prestige than the feminine because decisions taken in relation to affines would have determined and controlled those taken in relation to consanguine relatives (for example,

---

[7] About the possibility of this having happened to the Awá, see Balée (1994: 209–210). For other cases, there are good references in Politis (2007: 327–329) and Rival (1999).

Ortner and Whitehead 1981: 18; Turner 1979: 156). However, as I have noted in the case of the Awá, a greater prestige of the masculine does not necessarily imply any form of power or control over other group members or the slightest form of male domination over women.

All present-day data considered, it could be assumed that the mutual complementarity which defined the first hunter-gatherer societies need not have implied unequal power relationships between men and women. Should the term "gender" therefore be used when considering these societies? This is not an easy question. If by "gender" we mean a set of differences between men and women's identities which do not necessarily imply power relations, then perhaps gender does exist in these societies, as there are certain differences which stem from their respective functionally specialized tasks and the ensuing slight variations in mobility. If this is the case, then the correlation (so far considered universal) between gender and patriarchy should be discarded: situations may exist where gender differences imply differences of prestige but not of power. Therefore, in these cases—which only arise when there is neither functional division nor labor specialization with respect to group members of the same sex—gender relations do not necessarily imply the existence of a patriarchal order. These differences of prestige do, however, lay the foundations, the conditions, and the reasons for the logic of inequality that will eventually permeate the historical pathways of all known societies. Thus, two questions remain before continuing with our reasoning: (a) why should the masculine have acquired greater prestige if it does not necessarily involve a power relationship? (b) How could this bring about the clear positions of power and domination which are typical of the patriarchal order?

The answer to the first question has been set forth in the previous chapter. Differences in mobility, which in any hunter-gatherer society have enormous consequences on the construction of both identities, have gone hand in hand with the functions performed by men and women. As we have seen, in oral societies the world's limits are defined by the distances and territories that can be traveled on a daily basis. The rest of the universe does not exist, as it cannot be represented or imagined. So, if it can be assumed that, as in all present-day groups, the men took over those activities which involved covering longer distances and higher risks in order to protect a vulnerable offspring, they can also be assumed to have come to inhabit a slightly different world from women. The masculine world would have required a slightly greater ability to make decisions and to face the unknown and an almost imperceptibly greater emotional distance from the world. This constitutes the starting point of the process of individuation.

In those original societies, as with modern-day hunters, there would be no trace of individuation as known in later historical periods, when functional division and work specialization caused some to gradually begin to perceive themselves as different from the rest of the group. Such differences do not exist among hunter-gatherers and, as we have seen, the absence of technological control makes them unable to conceive of themselves apart from their own group. For this reason, while this can in no way be described as individuation, it could be said that the need to confront greater dangers and a slightly wider and more varied world than that inhabited by women may have put men in a better position to develop individuating features later on—possibly reinforcing the need to detach themselves from their mothers, as psychoanalysts argue. I am neither referring to hormonal determinants of any kind nor trying to use reductionist biological arguments, as I am completely convinced of the complexity and inextricable character of the interplay of nature and culture (a clear example of constant interaction and codetermination).[8] I do not deny that a biological difference between men and women could have been a part of this process, but if this had been the case, it could have been connected to the necessarily higher level of assertiveness that mobility required of men, in a relationship that is not of cause and effect but of mutual codetermination (such as the subject-object relationship I discussed previously). Bonobos (as opposed to common chimpanzees) demonstrate that when a social organization is not ruled by the sexual dimorphism of dominant males and there is no symbolic apprehension of the world, there will be no differences in the assertiveness and autonomy of its male and female members.

My hypothesis is that, in the early stages of history, men would have displayed slightly higher levels of curiosity, assertiveness, and decisiveness as a result of the relationship with the world implied by their higher mobility. Although these traits may have been expressed biologically too—through differentiated neuronal synapses, for example—they were caused by differences in mobility, and not the product of any socially unalterable biological essence. This way, gradually and imperceptibly at first, men would have been able to bring about minimal functional differences, or minimal changes in their decisions, which would have generated slight increases in their control over nature, enhancing feelings of security and difference from (and ultimately power over) those who did not have such control. In fact, the first positions of power signaled by the archaeological record coincide with the first evidence of technological control over nature, and both were embodied by men, as their burials suggest. This shows that power over nature is inextricably linked to power within a group, and both forms of power point to the earliest traces of individuation, because they were ultimately part of the same process: the process by which those persons who had material control of certain phenomena began to experience an emotional detachment from those phenomena which was associated both to power and to differentiation from the rest of the group. It was this very detachment that laid the foundations of an inner core that, in a later historical phase, came to constitute the self.

And yet, a second question remains: how could this have brought about power relations between the sexes historically? In the next few chapters, I intend to develop the arguments that will allow us to answer this question. But I would also like to highlight two fundamental aspects: (a) the gradual and imperceptible character of these changes in power relations in the early stages of history—an aspect which I consider crucial to our understanding of why women participated in dynamics

---

[8] The same point of view is shared by Fausto-Sterling (1985, 2000), Siegel (2012), Damasio (1994) and Walter (2010). Neurologist Shlain (1999) holds that men and women's brains would have been modeled in different ways as their social behaviors became increasingly different.

which eventually placed them in a position of subordination—and (b) that male domination and the subordination of women, as this began to appear once power differences emerged, were neither the direct consequences of differences between the sexes nor in any way connected to unjustifiable *a priori* values of each of their functions. Instead, these were rooted in the cognitive and identity implications of differences in mobility which characterized a certain pattern of functional complementarity, developed to look after an extremely dependent offspring. If differences in mobility disappear, so will the differences in identity construction. As I noted above, I think that mobility, not maternity, had the key role in the origin of differences between men and women's individuation levels.

References

Balée, W. (1994). *Footprints of the Forest. Ka'apor Ethnobotany. The Historical Ecology of Plant Utilization by an Amazonian People*. New York: Columbia University Press.
Beckerman, S., & Valentine, P. (Eds.). (2002). *Cultures of multiple fathers. The theory and practice of Partible Paternity in Lowland South America*. Miami: University of Florida Press.
Begler, E. B. (1978). Sex, status, and authority in Egalitarian society. *American Anthropologist (New Series), 80*(3), 571–588.
Campbell, A. T. (1989). *To square with genesis. Causal statements and shamanic ideas in Wayapí*. Iowa City: University of Iowa Press.
Chodorow, N. J. (1978). *The reproduction of mothering: Psychoanalysis and the sociology of gender*. Berkeley: University of California Press.
Cormier, L. A. (2003a). *Kinship with monkeys. The Guajá foragers of Eastern Amazonia*. Nueva York: Columbia University Press.
Cormier, L. A. (2003b). Decolonizing history. Ritual transformation of the past among the Guajá of Eastern Amazonia. In N. L. Whitehead (Ed.), *Histories and historicities in Amazonia* (pp. 123–139). Lincoln/Londres: University of Nebraska Press.
Cowell, A. (1973). *The tribe that hides from man*. Nueva York: Stein and Day Publishers.
Damasio, A. (1994). *Descartes' error*. New York: G.P. Putnam.
Descola, P. (2001). The genres of gender: Local models and global paradigms in the comparison of Amazonia and Melanesia. In T. Gregor & D. Tuzin (Eds.), *Gender in Amazonia and Melanesia* (pp. 91–114). Berkeley: University of California Press.
Dio Bleichmar, E. (1998). *La sexualidad femenina. De la niña a la mujer*. Paidós: Buenos Aires.
Eliade, M. (1959). *The sacred and the profane; the nature of religion*. New York: Harcourt, Brace & World.
Fausto, C. (1999). Of enemies and pets: Warfare and shamanism in Amazonia. *American Ethnologist, 26*, 933–956.
Fausto, C., & Viveiros de Castro, E. (1993). La puissance et l'acte: La parenté dans les basses terres de l'Amérique du Sud. *L'Homme* (126–128), 141–170.
Fausto-Sterling, A. (1985). *Myths of gender. Biological theories about women and men*. Nueva York: Basic Books.
Fausto-Sterling, A. (2000). *Sexing the body: Gender politics and the construction of sexuality*. New York: Basic Books.
Flanagan, J. G. (1989). Hierarchy in simple 'Egalitarian' societies. *Annual Review of Anthropology, 18*, 245–266.
Forline, L. C. (1997). The persistence and cultural transformations of the Guajá Indians: Foragers or Maranhão State, Brazil. PhD thesis, University of Florida, Gainesville.
Fried, M. H. (1967). *The evolution of political society*. Nueva York: Random House.

References

Gándara, M. (1990). La analogía etnográfica como heurística: lógica muestral, dominios ontológicos e historicidad. In Y. Sugiera & P. María Carmen Serra (Eds.), *Etnoarqueología. Coloquio Bosch Gimpera* (pp. 43–82). México: Universidad Nacional Autónoma de México.

Giddens, A. (1991). *Modernity and self identity: Self and society in Late Modern Age*. Cambridge: Polity Press.

González Ruibal, A., & Hernando, A. (2010). Genealogies of destruction. Archaeology of the contemporary past in the Amazonian forest, Archaeologies. *Journal of the World Archaeological Congress, 6*(1), 5–28.

Gow, P. (1989). The perverse child: Desire in a native Amazonian subsistence economy. *Man (New Series), 24*(4), 567–582.

Havelock, E. A. (1986). *The muse learns to write: Reflections on orality and literacy from antiquity to the present*. New Haven: Yale University Press.

Hernando, A. (2006). Arqueología y globalización. El problema de la definición del 'otro' en la postmodernidad. *Complutum, 17* (221–234).

Hernando, A., Politis, G., González Ruibal, A., & Coello, E. B. (2011). Gender, power and mobility among the Awá-Guajá (Maranhão, Brasil). *Journal of Anthropological Research, 67*(2), 189–211.

Hrdy, S. B. (1999). *The woman that never evolved*. Cambridge, MA: Harvard University Press.

Kent, S. (1993). Sharing in an egalitarian Kalahari community. *Man (New Series), 28*(3), 479–514.

Kozák, V., Baxter, D., Williamson, L., & Carneiro, R. L. (1979). *The Héta indians: fishing in a dry pond*. Nueva York: Anthropological Papers of the American Museum of Natural History (55:6).

Leacock, E. B. (1992). Women' status in egalitarian society. Implications for social evolution. *Current Anthropology, 33*(1), 225–259.

Lee, R. B. (1982). Politics, sexual and non-sexual, in an egalitarian society. In E. B. Leacock & R. B. Lee (Eds.), *Politics and history in band societies, Cambridge* (pp. 37–59). Cambridge: Cambridge University Press.

Leenhardt, M. (1979 [1947]). *Do Kamo: person and myth in the Melanesian world*. Chicago: University Press

Levinton, N. (2000). *El superyo femenino. La moral en las mujeres*. Madrid: Biblioteca Nueva.

MacCallum, C. (1990). Language, kinship and politics in Amazonia. *Man (New Series), 25*, 412–433.

Midgley, M. (2004). *The myths we live by*. Londres/New York: Routledge Classics.

Ong, W. (1982). *Orality and literacy. The technologizing of the word*. Londres: Routledge.

Ortner, S. B. (1996). *Making gender. The politics and erotics of culture*. Boston: Beacon Press.

Ortner, S. B., & Whitehead, H. (Eds.). (1981). *Sexual meanings: The cultural construction of gender and sexuality*. Cambridge: Cambridge University Press.

Politis, G. (2007). *Nukak. Ethnoarchaeology of an Amazonian People*. Walnut Creek: University College London Institute of Archaeology Publications.

Rival, L. (1999). Introduction: South America. In R. B. Lee & R. H. Daly (Eds.), *The Cambridge encyclopedia of hunters and gatherers* (pp. 77–85). Cambridge: Cambridge University Press.

Rival, L. (2005). The attachment of the soul to the body among the Huaorani of Amazonian Ecuador. *Ethnos, 70*(3), 285–310.

Rival, L. (2007). Proies Meurtrières, Rameaux Bourgeonnants: Masculinité et féminité en Terre Huaorani (Amazonie équatorienne). In N.-C. Mathieu (Ed.), *La Notion de personne femme et homme en dociétés matrilinéaires et Uxori-matrilocales* (pp. 125–154). París: Ed. Maison des Sciences de l'Homme.

Rogers, S. C. (1975). Female forms of power and the myth of male dominance. *American Ethnologist, 2*(4), 727–757.

Sanday, P. R. (1981). *Female power and male dominance. On the origins of sexual inequality*. Cambridge: Cambridge University Press.

Scott, J. (1986). Gender: A useful category of historical analysis. *American Historical Review, 91*, 1053–1075.

Seymour-Smith, C. (1991). Women have no affines and men no kin: The politics of the Jivaroan Gender Relation. *Man (New Series), 26*(4), 629–649.

Shlain, L. (1999). *The alphabet versus the Goddess. The conflict between word and image*. Nueva York: Penguin/Compass.

Siegel, D. J. (2012). *The developing mind: how relationships and the brain interact to shape who we are*. New York: Guilford Press.

Silva, M. (2001). Relações de gênero entre os Enawene-Nawe. *Tellus, 1*(1), 41–65.

Turner, T. S. (1979). The Gê and Bororo Societies as dialectical systems: A general model. In D. Maybury-Lewis & J. Bamberger (Eds.), *Dialectical societies: The Gê and Bororo of Central Brazil* (pp. 147–178). Cambridge, MA: Harvard University Press.

Vilaça, A. (2002). Making kin out of Others in Amazonia. *Journal of the Royal Anthropological Institute, 8*(2), 347–365.

Viveiros de Castro, E. (1992). *From the enemy's point of view. Humanity and divinity in an Amazonian Society*. Chicago: The University of Chicago Press.

Walter, N. (2010). *Living dolls: The return of sexism*. London: Virago.

Zent, E.L. (2006). *Morar en la selva: humanidad, prescripciones y seres hipostáticos entre los Hotï, Guayana venezolana* (Working Paper N° 19). Latin American Studies Center, College Park, The University of Maryland.

Chapter 5
Individuality (or Identity When One Has Power over the World)

Let us turn now to the opposite end of the process of cultural transformation being described in these pages—and the ensuing identity transformations—to better understand the defining features of both. Let us take as an example a person occupying a specialized position of power in a group as socioeconomically complex as the postindustrial society we live in. Let us consider the way in which such persons construct their identity.

Although there are many different possible points of view from which to analyze power (Lukes 2005), most would agree with Norbert Elias' (1991: 52) definition of power as "the expression of a particularly great capacity to influence the self-direction and the fate of other people." This means that in order to wield power, one must, first, have in mind a clear course of action for oneself and for the destinies of those others. This, in turn, requires great awareness of one's own desires and the necessary self-confidence to grant these more importance than theirs. Wielding power thus requires a certain degree of individuation and the ability to objectify those things or persons over which it is exercised. One must take on a *subject* position in a relationship where others become the *objects* of one's own desires. It means objectifying the world, rationalizing it, and placing oneself at an emotional distance from it. For this reason, whenever we successfully bring a natural phenomenon under control, not only do we gain a certain level of power but also a certain level of individuation (as something which had so far been considered human now becomes objectified, causing a loss of personal relationship).

As societies become increasingly divided in their functions and labor specialization, their individual members' personal trajectories also become more diversified. Processes of social division mean that individuals develop skills which require different capacities of knowledge and control. As a result, they rightly begin to perceive themselves as different from each other, as in fact they are increasingly becoming so. At the same time, as they perceive this increase in their own individuation, everyday social dynamics gradually force each one of them to engage with a growing number of other people. These others fulfill tasks complementary to one's own but rarely establish emotional relationships with one. Reflecting on this,

Norbert Elias (1987, 1991, 1994) pointed out how, as social functions multiplied historically, people automatically and unconsciously became more and more used to modulating the extent to which they expressed their emotions. In a society as socioeconomically complex as our own, we all depend on each other to survive. And every day we interact with many others on varying levels of emotional connection: we get up and interact with our relatives (if we happen to have a family). We get on the bus and greet the driver (if we are polite and although we might not know them). Then, we arrive at work and interact with our colleagues, with whom we may have established a kind but not necessarily intimate relationship (or an unpleasant but daily one). We also interact with our boss, who we may or may not like, but on whom our job depends. After work we might go for a beer with our friends, with whom we share varying degrees of trust and intimacy. We greet the waiter, who may know us if we are bar regulars, but with whom we have yet another different relationship from the one we have with our friends. A quick count of the number of people we interact with throughout the day shows just how accustomed we have become to automatically adjusting the emotions we express when engaging in a society with high functional division and work specialization.

This ability to mask our emotions in other people's presence is the result of increased personal individualization. In a society like ours, social interaction requires an incredibly wide scope of relationship levels, imposing the need to hide our feelings toward other group members, especially where these could turn out detrimental to the relationship itself. As a present-day example, imagine a situation where we despised a boss or a teacher, but where we could only ever express this at the risk of their disapproval and the possibility that we might lose our job or fail our exams. Obviously, caution would advise us to make our own lives easier by hiding the emotions that this relationship fills us with. This type of precaution, which has increasingly come to characterize our everyday lives, is the historical counterpart of increased socioeconomic complexity. It was Elias' opinion that this leads to yet another shared realization: if we do not always express our feelings freely in other people's presence—sometimes even expressing the opposite for the sake of our own interests—then others might behave in the same way toward ourselves. We become aware of our own unawareness of what others might really feel when they interact with us. As socioeconomic complexity and the subsequent scientific knowledge increase, so does the potential threat posed by each person to the rest of us. This is one of the key aspects of what Elias famously called the *civilizing process*, where, he stated (Elías 1994: 497) "inner fears grow in proportion to the decrease of outer ones."

Over the course of history, as socioeconomic complexity increased, so did the need for group members to repress their feelings toward others. Ironically, this has also caused us to become more and more aware of the very existence of these troublesome feelings. Such is the origin of the very idea of the "self," that alleged internal core bearing the sum total of what we feel and are, and which we share with others in varying proportions, but never in its entirety. This concept of an *individual*—associated with the idea of "I"—did not exist in classical times. While it was used in Medieval Latin, it did not yet refer to people. The term individual used to designate exclusively something indivisible and inseparable from a whole set of other entities, which is what the terms *individualis* or *individuus* mean (Elias 1991: 160–1). The few undoubted examples of highly individuated people in the ancient world were always associated with abstract thought and writing and were exceptions to the norm in their own social context. In the eleventh and twelfth centuries, as a result of the appearance of the first *bourgeois* (inhabitants of the burgs, the first urban centers) and of the spread of writing brought about by Christianity, the men in these social groupings began to cultivate a form of identity defined by certain individuating features (Morris 1987; Hernando 2002). The twelfth century also saw the appearance of the first Western universities, which were specifically devised as exclusively male locales (Schiebinger 1989: 13–14) for men's training in proficient abstract and rational thinking. Still, this type of identity only came to aptly describe a majority of men in the seventeenth century. At that point, society attained a level of functional division which opened up the possibility of truly individual personal trajectories for each one of its members. As men became *empowered*, they divested God from more of His power and took control over their destinies into their own hands. By the seventeenth century, they had begun to consider themselves *individuals*, isolated and self-sufficient instances of identity. It was then that the term *individual* became equated with the term *person* (Mauss 1968; Elias 1991: 161).[1]

In the nineteenth century, a great number of men already engaged in the world through individuality and its mechanisms (reason, technology, etc.). At this point, they were numerous enough to mobilize a social discourse which replaced the *truth* of myth for that of science. Thus, the importance of the sacred, its permanence and recurrence, gave way to the power of change and reason. Lyell's *Principles of Geology* (1830–1833) proved that the Earth itself had a long history of gradual changes. Darwin applied the idea to his own theory of evolution (1859). He contended that the natural species had not been created by God in their exact extant forms. Instead, animals were the result of changes brought on by complexity, the product of increasingly diversified gradual transformations which had followed a natural logic, a logic that could now be explained through reason. At first, Darwin struggled to include human beings in his theory, and it was only in 1871 that his *The Descent of Man, and Selection in Relation to Sex* clearly stated that our own appearance too could be explained separately from God, definitively granting human beings autonomy from the sacred instance. At around the same time, in 1848, Marx and Engels published their *Communist Manifesto*, where contemporary society was explained through change. By the 1880s, Freud had started publishing his own psychoanalytic version of individual subjectivity, which, contrary to other psychological explanations, placed the past and time at the very center of his interpretation. Social discourse came to transform some of the most profound principles which had governed it so far and began to enshrine change as a key to our own survival and *superiority*. Indeed, around this time, even the discourse about our origins began to revolve around time: myth was altogether replaced by history as the means to

---

[1] I am grateful to Laura Freixas for pointing out to me that the first known *intimate diary* was written by the English civil servant and politician Samuel Pepys between 1660 and 1669.

construe our own past. The past itself was displaced from other *spaces* (such as Heaven, Hell, or Purgatory) to be anchored in the ever-changing *other times* of our history. Ever since, modern humans have understood the world through individuality, reason, and change. These foundations may appear universal to us, and even pertaining to the very intrinsic essence of humanity, but are actually truly particular and specific. In fact, individuality is associated exclusively with people with a high level of rational understanding and a certain level of material and technological control over reality.

The result of a complex historical process itself, individuality developed alongside other historical trends, such as increased technological control over the world and rational explanations of it. Individuality stems from the emotional distance opened up between a person and what they can control or know through reason. It is also the result of the interpersonal and intragroup differences brought about by the development of technology and labor specialization. The individuating process is thus the effect of increased socioeconomic complexity on identity construction, whether or not writing has been invented. But there are limits to the level of technological control over the world that oral societies can attain—and to their ability to provide rational explanations for its phenomena. Oral societies lack the abstract or scientific formulae to represent the recurrences and mechanisms of natural phenomena, which also impose limits on the level of individuation they can reach. Therefore, once oral societies had reached the highest possible levels of objectification, technological control and individuation in each historical process, their—incipiently—individuated men took up a new "intellectual technology,"[2] writing, which allowed both them and society to channel the trend of increased complexity and individuation. Although not automatically, writing triggered technological control, rational explanations, and individuality. As mentioned above, Facebook and Zuckerberg provide useful parallels for the dynamics which most likely gained momentum at this stage. It is precisely because society presents certain characteristics that people are socialized in certain ways (or trends). They then develop the material culture and technology to satisfy the demands generated by that society, in turn transforming the socialization patterns of future generations. These "intellectual technologies" can have transcendent (and unplanned) long-term consequences as they radically transform the way in which any given society understands the world and its own place in it—i.e., the way in which it construes identity. Writing is an excellent case in point. Once developed, its potential transformed individuation levels and people's capacity to yield power in the world so radically that, as we shall see, women's access to this new intellectual technology was carefully prevented until the arrival of modernity.

Although I will not go into the topic of writing in depth,[3] it does have to be stated, at least, that writing is a radical mechanism of individuation. Writing allows us to

---

[2] A concept used by Ong (1982: 81–83) and Goody (2000) to refer to writing, and which Carr (2010: 44) has taken up to apply to the Internet.

[3] The works of Ong (1982), Olson (1994) or Havelock (1986) provide in-depth explanations of the fundamental differences in the ways of thinking associated with orality and writing. Rodríguez Mayorgas (2010) competently reviews the appearance of the second. More extensive literature can be found in Hernando (2002).

break up our relationship with the world into two levels: the rational, through representations of it, and the emotional, through personal contact. The latter, while already existing in oral societies, remains a part of the lives of all literate individuals, in the form of lived relationships. Olson (1994) called the type of signs used by oral societies to represent reality *metonymic* because their signs are an integral part of the reality they intend to represent. A person's name, for example, is part of their spirit, whereas by writing it down, a name can be visualized as a separate entity from the person themselves, a mere label operating on a representational level. For the same reason, signs used to represent the sacred are in themselves sacred too, making it a sin to *use God's name in vain* or to attack the image of a saint. Unlike written representations (which Olson calls *metaphoric*), in myth representation becomes part of the very reality being named.

Writing, on the other hand, splits reality into two different levels: one for reality itself and the other for its representation. This makes it possible for someone to engage with the latter and not the former. Thus, we are capable, for example, of imagining the concept of a tree without having to imagine any tree in particular (like a lemon tree, a pear tree, a pine tree). Or, we can imagine the concept of a circle without having to picture any natural elements with this shape (such as the sun, or a wheel). Our relationship with the world can be established on a rational level which excludes the emotional. To those of us who use writing, this level of reflection can seem misleadingly intrinsic to thought itself, but this entire realm is completely absent from both oral societies and the illiterate people within literate groups.

When carrying out fieldwork among the Awá, our team was forced to become fully aware of the absence of this dissociation from their thought. We realized that it was impossible, for example, to ask about the meaning of specific words or about the way of constructing certain expressions. The Awá cannot possibly analyze the logic of their language, for "language" does not exist for them as something to reflect on. They cannot conceive of an abstract level of language made up of rules, words, morphemes, and suffixes. Or we understood that our merely curious questions about whether they might be going out hunting the next day would ring offensive in their ears. Such questions were met with restless, defensive, and clearly uneasy responses. It wasn't long before we realized that we could not simply make that kind of questions. Since the Awá (as any oral society) always link thought to concrete action, asking whether they would go out hunting the next day would put pressure on them to actually do so. It was as if a manager asked an employee, "are you delivering that parcel tomorrow?" or if a mother asked her child "have you washed your hands?" There is no such thing as abstract thought dissociated from action in orality and no awareness of the mind, or verbs that refer to mental states—such as to think, to decide, to believe, to doubt, to confuse, etc. (Olson 1994: 238; see also Ong 1982; Havelock 1986). Of course, oral societies can dissociate reason from emotion for those phenomena which they can control (for if they can, this is precisely because their dynamics have, to some extent, been deciphered and are no longer considered human). But they cannot possibly conceive of general laws to represent the way in which different phenomena operate, as this requires science and the use of writing. This means that in orality, it is not possible to set a separate level of representation of the world apart from firsthand personal or lived experience.

To summarize, people who use writing engage with the phenomena they experience personally on two different levels. First, on the level that engages with these through emotions and in the exact same way as oral societies. Second, on the level that engages with them through reason. To illustrate this, I will use as an example the excellent advertisement of a well-known watch brand shown on Spanish television. The advert asked viewers, "how long does a minute last?" and showed several different human situations: some boring and tiresome, others cheerful and stimulating, some painful, others exciting, some desired, and others undesirable. A small rubric was superimposed on them with how long a single minute *seemed to last* in each one of them. The objective knowledge of how long a minute lasts is not the same as our subjective perception of its duration. The same is true about the spatial perception of places where we have experienced important episodes in our lives, as the scenery of happy childhood holidays, for example. These landscapes can be represented through the two dimensions of a map, their extension and distances can be calculated. But their dimensions will multiply when we return to them and remember the meanings and emotions that became attached to each tree, to every stone, to each road, river, or beach, all of which are part of the scenery of memories that have shaped us as people and made us who we are. A person with a strictly oral cultural background can only perceive reality in this subjective and emotional dimension, but writing expands perception and introduces a level which is intrinsically associated with power over the event represented. By writing, we take on the agent position, the position of a subject who understands the nonhuman dynamics governing the represented phenomenon. This, added to the fact that knowledge is not transmitted through personal relationships as in oral cultures, but through isolation and abstraction (Ong 1982: 71–2), gradually increases the sense of individuality and power.

And yet, this power not only stems from the emotional detachment from known and lived events. Whereas oral cultures only gain knowledge over those phenomena which have been experienced personally (or which someone in the group has experienced and described), writing enables relationships with as many sets of events as can be represented by decodable formulae. This means that writing extends the boundaries of the world and reality, to include anything that has previously been encoded: not only other spaces and times we have not witnessed personally but also animals, cultures, people, bacteria, or black holes which we will never be able to see firsthand. Writing causes the world to explode, to widen and gain depth, to diversify, and color up before the excited and empowered eyes of whoever can read it, because the very act of reading the world provides a sense of control. Historically, the "intellectual technology" of writing meant a quantum leap in the process of technological control, rationalization, and individuation that had already begun to characterize human development during prehistory.

Given the position of power and agency it grants those who can establish it, the scientific/rational relationship acquired increasing social visibility, a visibility that was coherent with the gradual masking of the emotional worlds of those people who took part in increasingly complex interactions and were increasingly individualized. Writing eventually became, then, the perfect vehicle for the dissociation between reason and emotion that had already emerged among those who exerted power and technological control over society. (Or we could say that, given the always intertwined nature of relationships between cultural elements, writing was also the product of such dissociation).

To summarize the structural traits of this process, we could say that the construction of individuality—that is, the identification of the concepts of individual and person—culminated, by spreading to a vast majority of men, in the seventeenth century. At the same time, two other closely related concepts were gaining relevance: the concept of *risk* (signaling those individuals' dare and desire for change) and a new definition of *being* which equated it to abstract thought and enshrined the existence of the mind—remember Descartes' well-known *cogito ergo sum* (Olson 1994:243). As the process unfolded, the dissociation of reason and emotion and the idealization of reason continued to increase until they were finally consolidated by enlightened thought in the eighteenth century.

The fact is that men were progressively caught in the traps of this process, because as change became a precondition for their security, anxiety became more and more central in the type of identity they were increasingly socialized into. Ever since that moment, men would not only seek change for its greater social importance but also as a prerequisite for their own self-esteem and sense of security. The higher the position of power these men occupied, the more individuated they became, and the more value they placed on change as a key for their own security. This would force them, first, to have a clear view of the direction they wished to give those changes and therefore, a consciousness of their own wishes, together with a clear will to struggle to satisfy them. Such are the requirements of the sense of security promised by the self and change. All the authors who have studied individuality thus agree that one of its defining features is *reflexivity*, a unified awareness of oneself and of the coherence guiding self-transformation (Veyne 1987: 7; Giddens 1991: 20, 52; Weintraub 1978: 95). In individuality, security is not gained from satisfying the desires of the Other, but from generating, recognizing, pursuing, and satisfying one's own desires for oneself (see a summary of these traits in Fig. 5.1).

Modernity, the state of culture brought on by the Industrial Revolution (Giddens 1991: 15), and which as a historical phase signals the highest levels of all the features mentioned (science, technological control, and masculine individualization), was erected, then, on two complementary and contradictory categories with strong implications in terms of identity: first, on the objectification of a technologically controlled world, that is, on scientific knowledge, based on universal reason, and second, on the individuality as the form of identity, with its reflective counterpart, subjectivity. Within it, a core of repressed emotions is concentrated which, while remaining unspoken, plays a fundamental role in our relationships with the world.

High division of functions and work specialization
Diversified and changing activities
Nonhuman nature is seen as obeying its own dynamics: SCIENCE
Abstract-rational engagement with a number of natural elements which no emotional relationship is established with.
Nonhuman nature is not (consciously) perceived as a threat felt (because it is controlled/understood)
Fear of human nature (caused by highly differentiated behaviors)
INDIVIDUAL IDENTITY: Its core lies is in the individual "self"
Change is positively valued
Time constitutes the most visible axis in the organization of reality
FEELS POWERFUL IN THE WORLD
Trust in destiny and survival is placed in personal work and initiative
Security is based on being the agent of controlled action: SUBJECT position
Personal identity manifests itself through the conscience of one's own desires and ability to satisfy them

Fig. 5.1 Structural traits of INDIVIDUALITY

Both universal reason and individuality are intrinsically associated with a feeling of power: the more capable we are of rationalizing the world, the more individuated and capable of wielding power we become. And in the Western world, all these features have increasingly been embodied by men. Historical accounts describe this development as having happened independently of emotional dynamics, since, ascribing to the view that they have little to do with the dynamics of reason, researchers fail to take the former into consideration. This *denial* of the emotional dynamics that accompanied the process of rationalization and individuation lies at the deepest core of the discourse into which we are socialized in, which we teach in our history classes and hand down to our children. It is the discourse that constitutes us, weaving the veil through which we all learn to look at the world and ourselves from the very moment we are born. As a society, we idealize reason and *deny* the importance of emotions, and we even look down on public displays of these.

My contention is that it is this very *denial*, enshrined as the *truth* by enlightened thought, and sustained by the individuated men and some women of modernity—because it is the key to admittance into power circuits (political, scientific, academic, economic)—, that constitutes the most profound insight into male domination over women.

The reason is that individuality—as described here—is, in emotional terms, a highly costly identity mode. Since change comes to define existence, individuality causes the constant feeling of anxiety brought on by our permanent state of never having *fully become*. Achievements are never enough; we are permanently dissatisfied, and, since we live in constant need of change in order to remain secure about ourselves, our aspirations become insatiable. Also, the more individuality defines the identities of those in command, the more society will be defined by change (let us not forget fractal relationships). People will not only experience the subjective need to change but also an objective, social demand for it if they aspire to the rewards of success and power. People will be constantly impelled to change, innovate, advance, and never stop generating new ideas. Without perhaps understanding the purpose of all this, and although deep down inside they might wish to stop and *drop out* of this over-accelerated world, they will be insatiably challenged to renovate technologies, relationships, and phases in their own lives.

At the same time, and as part of the same process, as society and our personal lives are increasingly defined by change, more and more phenomena will be understood scientifically and controlled technologically, and less will be explained in human terms. This means that the more natural phenomena we can explain, the less human or personal relationships will be established with them. Thus, as the result of their increasingly rational understanding of the world, human beings become more and more lonely. They are left without protective gods, facing a universe that unfolds independently of their groups and which they can no longer understand as a projection of their own group dynamics. Understanding how this world works can be empowering, but it is also emotionally stranding and leaves a cold and metallike aftertaste. Power always takes an emotional toll. As he wondered about how human beings had managed to pay this price throughout history, Norbert Elias (1987: 68) guessed that the emotional loss was probably compensated by a sense of dominion and control over natural phenomena.

In the following pages, I will contend that to unveil the patriarchal order's trappings, we must understand that *that (emotional) price was never paid, because it cannot possibly be paid.* If human beings had actually freed themselves from their groups (as the idea of individuality assumes) and if they had effectively stopped connecting to their world through emotion (as autonomous reason claims), the entire process wouldn't have taken place in the first place. Had this been the case, the security gained by human beings through reason would have been countered by the much greater insecurity caused by awareness of their obvious minuteness and impotence in the face of an inevitably uncontrollable universe. And this would have deterred them from effecting any more changes. If in fact the process of increased individuation and reason took place with the characteristics, rhythm, and progression it did, that was because the men who embodied that identity developed mechanisms to avoid becoming increasingly isolated, to retain a feeling of stability in the midst of rapid change, and to maintain the warmth of emotions in the cold draft they felt coming in through the open doors of reason. These mechanisms prevented them from paying the emotional price of increased reason, and remain part of an untold history, hidden and masked by social discourse, because those who have historically developed individuality and reason have never recognized their importance. Men have never recognized these mechanisms because they themselves were incapable of seeing them, increasingly hidden as these remained within the subjectivity they had gradually built as the counterpart of their rational relationship with the world.

In the next few pages, I set out to analyze the way in which *denial* has been effectively constituted from the point of view of identity. My aim is to explain, first, why the subordination of women is a precondition of an order based on the *fantasy of individuality* and of autonomous reason and, secondly, why no struggle for equality can ever be effective unless it moves on from discussing reasons to reclaiming the value of emotions.

With an archaeologist's gaze, I shall direct my attention to what those male individuated (and patriarchally minded) masters of science, technology, and reason enact—and not just to what social discourse says they do. By doing so, we can begin to uncover new dimensions of what has always been in front of our eyes but which remained unseen through the spectrum of the dominant social discourse. Only by uncovering what this discourse hides and what remained unacknowledged because it had been so concealed that we gaze at it unseeingly, can we grasp the full dimension of the fantasy of individuality, a fantasy upholding an order which claims to have successfully excluded emotions from its security mechanisms.

References

Carr, N. (2010). *The shallows: What the Internet is doing to our brains*. New York: W.W. Norton.
Elias, N. (1987). *Involvement and detachment*. Oxford: Blackwell.
Elias, N. (1991). *The Society of Individuals*. London: Basil Blackweell.
Elías, N. (1994). *The civilizing process. The history of manners and state formation and civilization*. Oxford: Blackwell.
Giddens, A. (1991). *Modernity and self identity: Self and society in late modern age*. Cambridge: Polity Press.
Goody, J. (2000). *The power of the written tradition*. Washington/Londres: Smithsonian Institution Press.
Havelock, E. A. (1986). *The muse learns to write: Reflections on orality and literacy from antiquity to the present*. New Haven: Yale University Press.
Hernando, A. (2002). *Arqueología de la Identidad*. Madrid: Akal.
Lukes, S. (2005). *Power: A radical view*. New York: Palgrave Macmillan.
Mauss, M. (1968) [1950]. A category of the human spirit. *Psychoanalitical Review, 55*, 457–481.

References

Morris, C. (1987). *The discovery of the individual. 1050–1200*. Toronto: University of Toronto Press/Medieval Academy of America.

Olson, D. R. (1994). *The world on paper. The conceptual and cognitive implication of writing and reading*. Cambridge: Cambridge University Press.

Ong, W. (1982). *Orality and literacy. The technologizing of the word*. Londres: Routledge.

Rodríguez Mayorgas, A. (2010). *Arqueología de la palabra*. Barcelona: Bellaterra.

Schiebinger, L. (1989). *The mind has no sex? Women in the origins of modern science*. Cambridge, MA: Harvard University Press.

Veyne, P. (1987). L'individu atteint au coeur par la pussance publique. In P. Veyne et al. (Eds.), *Colloque de Royaumont Sur l'individu* (pp. 7–19). París: Édition du Seuil.

Weintraub, K. (1978). *The value of the individual: Self and circumstance in autobiography*. Chicago: University of Chicago Press.

Chapter 6
Relational Identity/Individuated Identity: The Appearance of Things

Some 15 years ago (Hernando 2000), I identified the identity historically shared by women until modernity with *relational identity*. I also associated *individuality* with the identity mode which has gradually and progressively become identified with men, and I proposed that the arrival of modernity in the Western world had forced women to learn to cope with both modes of identity, causing a series of contradictions and conflicts which shall be analyzed in some detail in Chap. 7. But what I failed to see then were the contradictions and conflicts which I now find so blatantly inherent to the individuated identities of men. The reason I could not detect these contradictions was that, while the conflicts defining contemporary women's identities are, for the most part, fully acknowledged by them (and therefore socially visible), those defining contemporary men are not. Men's contradictions and conflicts are enacted unconsciously and excluded from a discourse (of *truth*), which leaves no space whatsoever for the workings of their own subjectivity. This discourse which, while masking the contradictions of male individuality, exposes only those of female individuality, is the *patriarchal discourse*. As a way of understanding and reflecting reality, it is based on the fantasy that any single human being can feel (and have) power over the world without feeling the need of belonging to a community. Throughout history, this fantasy of potency has provided the basis for both male individuality and the type of knowledge that has become associated with it: positive science. To understand how it has been made possible to uphold this fantasy, we must turn to the way in which human identity has been constructed in our own historical trajectory. This complex process operated on both a conscious and visible level and on an unconscious and *denied* level (which grew more and more as the pretensions of individuality became more ambitious). In this chapter I will deal with the first level, where individuality would appear to have replaced relational identity. First, we must tackle the *acknowledged* and the *conscious*, to understand later the hidden trappings which it carefully *denied* and which can be rendered visible only by abandoning social discourse. In the next two chapters, we will be able to scrutinize this second, unconscious and *denied* level.

6.1 The Historical Construction of Identity

A gradual acceleration of the changes defining the reality we live in (Virilio 2005; Bauman 2007; Sennett 1998) has caused an awakening interest in the social sciences. Rapid transformations increase our urge to understand identity, to find out what we are, and to establish how we human beings can define ourselves in a world where nothing can afford to both *remain* and retain its value. Contemporary research into personal identity provides two clearly defined positions:

(a) The first holds that, although there have been different types of identity throughout history, each person is to be considered an "individual" regardless of cultural specificity. This position rests on the assumption that any one person's self-experience is nontransferrable and unrepeatable, and yet, this constitutes in itself a universal trait of human nature.[1]

(b) The second position defends the existence of two historically different forms of identity: modern Western individuated identity and nonindividual nonmodern identity, commonly known as collective or relational identity.[2] In the latter, people do not perceive clear boundaries between themselves and other members of their own groups and construct their identities in ways that are "interdependent" (Markus and Kitayama 1991) or "dividual" (Bird-David 1999; Fowler 2005), through the mechanisms that Marilyn Strathern (1988) called "partibility" and "dividuality." From this point of view, only those who are part of modernity would be true "individuals."

It must be highlighted, however, that the main authors of reference for both perspectives agree that personal identity can present a combination of relational and individual traits,[3] although none of them consider the possibility that any general rule could explain particular combinations or sets of identity traits. As I see it, however, such a rule does exist.

In my view, relational and individuated identity constitutes two *separate blocks or sets* of traits which coexist *within the same person* in different percentages and which operate to varying degrees on the conscious level (the unconscious shall be dealt with below). These degrees depend on the capacity that each person has to control the world's phenomena and to explain them rationally. When people *cannot control* a certain phenomenon, they relate to it through their *relational identity*. But when they can control it, their relationship with this phenomenon is defined by the

---

[1] Among these authors are Sampson (1988), Cohen (1994), Ewing (1990), Moore (2000), Knapp and Meskell (1997), Knapp and Van Dommelen (2008), Machin (2009), Sökefeld (1999), etcetera.

[2] As espoused by Dumont (1986), Geertz (1984), Read (1955), Price-Williams (1980), or Thomas (2004).

[3] This opinion is also shared by LiPuma (2000), Kashima et al. (1995), Shweder and Bourne (1982), and Spiro (1993). Fowler (2016: 397) has recently worked on the "tension between individual and dividual aspects of personhood", declaring that "personhood is always relational" (although individuality may exist), "but in varied ways".

6.1 The Historical Construction of Identity

traits of *individuality*. This means that if a person can rationally control/explain many phenomena, their individuated identity will take up a high percentage of their whole personal identity. But if they have little control or scientific knowledge, then relational identity will hold a greater share of their personal identity. I will elaborate on this.

At the start of all historical trajectories, when there was no technological control whatsoever over the world nor any knowledge of its causal dynamics (both these intellectual developments took place simultaneously), all group members, both male and female, engaged in all real phenomena through relational identity. Thus, all phenomena were explained through human dynamics and attributed a sacred power, and the (sacred) instances created in that process were made the *subjects* of wishes that the human group should accomplish as a precondition for their own survival. All group members took on an *object* position toward these higher instances and defined themselves exclusively through the human relations they were socially interwoven into (I am my son's father, my nephew's uncle, etc.). The people in those groups relied on that sense of group belonging for the necessary strength to face up to a world, which they perceived as dominated by phenomena beyond their control. In this sense, I state that groups without any division of functions or work specialization maintain a *relational identity*.

Throughout history, as a growing number of the mechanisms of natural phenomena were controlled/explained, those capable of controlling/understanding them began to establish relationships with them through individuality, although their relationship with those phenomena they still failed to control or understand remained defined by relational identity. This means, for example, that as soon as people become familiar enough with the mechanics of plant growth to be able to intensify production—by the use of irrigation systems, fertilizer dung, or ploughs—they will no longer perceive the Earth as a sacred and powerful instance, but as a mere natural phenomenon, one which is different from human nature and whose logic they have deciphered and is therefore amenable to control. At this moment, individuated identity traits begin to mediate relationships with it: an emotional distance is kept from the Earth, for it is no longer considered human, and because its functioning has been understood, it no longer poses a threat. In this situation, people feel that they have power over it and not vice-versa, and their decisions and desires will shape the new relationship. This, in turn, will cause them to continue to generate successive changes, because their experience of having changed in the past will have increased their present material security. What happened in our own historical trajectory is that as a greater number of phenomena became controlled, those who developed that control and knowledge came to relate to more and more phenomena through the defining features of individuality, catalyzing what we call the *individuation process*.

I would like to clarify that I do not consider this process to have come about as a gradual transition from the features of relational identity to those of individual identity. I believe that both *blocks and sets* of traits always present themselves in full swing, for their respective defining features are structurally and necessarily connected. Therefore, if any single one of the features defining either set appears, we can expect all the other traits of that set to reveal themselves promptly, in high gear and in full swing. What *does* appear to varying degrees is the extent to which each *block* or *set* makes up each person's identity. This depends on the number of phenomena they can explain or control: the greater the scientific control or knowledge, the higher the percentage level of the individuality *block*.

To further clarify this point, I will give an example from our own culture: let us imagine an astrophysics professor—trained in a particularly abstract and rational academic discipline—whose very expertise and highly developed intellect allows him or her to establish rational relationships with most phenomena of reality, fully aware as they are of these phenomena's causal dynamics. Their identity will therefore be strongly individuated. In fact, it may be completely individuated on the conscious level if they consider themselves fully capable of explaining all the phenomena in the world they inhabit. And yet, they might still feel the need to answer a question for which the rational explanation could turn out to be insufficient: "What happens after death?" Within our world, it is only very rarely that our own deaths are accepted without any distress, as individuality places us at the center of our own universes. A purely rational answer to the question would limit itself to: "Nothing, nothing happens. Death is just a part of life, its full stop, and its end." But this individual might require a more consoling answer. An answer that might help him or her mitigate the anguish caused by the uncontrollable character of death. And, if this is the case, we will find our highly rational astrophysics professor compelled to resort to the mythic mechanisms of relational identity to answer this question. As a result, while interacting with the rest of reality in an abstract and rational way, they will rely, for this particular aspect, on mythical knowledge (let us say, for example, the Catholic one). Therefore, they will consider the dynamics of death to be governed by a sacred instance, created in the image and likeness of the (in this case patriarchal) social order; they will participate in a world where the past is read in spatial terms (Heaven, Hell, Purgatory) and where security is attained exclusively by knowing and satisfying the desires of the only subject ("I am he who is"), that is, the divinity, which they will recognize through the practice of certain rituals (such as mass or prayer). Regarding this phenomenon, the astrophysicist will consider themselves a mere part of a community (of believers) where they have no individual importance or power, as it will be through belonging to that community that they feel protected from the anguish that would otherwise overwhelm them. This example illustrates how the relational set of identity features can retain the same strength it would have in a group of hunter-gatherers. The only difference would be that, while the latter apply these to all of reality's phenomena, our astrophysicist relies on the relational identity set to grapple with the single phenomenon he, as yet, cannot fully understand and control—death.

The example of the astrophysics professor encapsulates the very foundations of the individuation process: historically, the identity counterpart of greater material control over the world was that a growing number of men felt power/control/knowledge over an increased number of phenomena, and the percentage of individuality in the construction of their identities increased accordingly. Eventually, having arrived at the Enlightenment and modernity, they acquired such high levels of knowledge and control over world dynamics that an altogether new phenomenon took place: never before in the entire history of all known human groups had it ever been possible for some of their members to discard the possibility of a god and to recognize themselves as atheists, that is, to *pretend that a protective instance was not needed* to feel safe in the world, and that reason and technology could be relied on so that individuals could generate that sense of security for themselves. (Let us bear in mind, once again, that this chapter is concerned only with the conscious part of identity, that is, the part that is recognized and made visible.)

Understanding what I have proposed here means accepting that the identities of the members of any social group can be as varied as the different possible positions of power within it. As the division of functions multiplied, the range of variation in different people's levels of individuation grew wider within the social group: all hunter-gatherers have a relational identity; but farmers who intensify production begin to present some internal variation corresponding to different levels of (even very slight) individuation. And once specialized activities begin to appear—such as metallurgy, trade, or crafts—this variation widens in correlation with the development of knowledge and control over these spheres and, therefore, with emerging positions of power. At the time when these activities first appeared, the percentage of individuation/control of those people (overwhelmingly mostly men) who carried them out was enough to allow them to feel different from the rest of their group. This was first made visible by the contents of their graves toward 2.500 B.C., as shall be explained below. It was then that chiefs first appeared, and their power (and individuation) continued to increase as they went on to control and rationally explain more of the world's phenomena. This was the reason why, as described in Chap. 5, writing caused individuation to peak.

This means that, wherever socioeconomic complexity increases, three other aspects will also inevitably grow: (a) the degree (percentage) of individuation that defines the most powerful members of the group, (b) the number of people with some degree of individuation/power, and (c) the range of individuation levels between different group members, in correlation with the variation in their level of power. People without the slightest level of individuation (leaving aside women, whom we shall turn to below) remain at the bottom of society and make up the majority of its illiterate and unskilled members. This means that the degree of individuation is correlated with that of function specialization and each individual person's level of power, since all three are merely different manifestations of the same dynamics which, until the arrival of modernity, were embodied only by men and not by women.

Let us turn back to an example from our own society: I have described a hypothetical astrophysics professor whose engagement with the world through the wealth of scientific knowledge makes them highly individuated. But the dynamics described could likewise apply to a ruler in political power or a millionaire with economic power. Control and expertise in their respective areas also have a powerful individuating effect on them, possibly leading us to conclude that our society is a highly individuated one. But what if we were to imagine an old peasant from the rural region of Galicia instead? A person who has never learned to read or write and possesses no other skills but the ability to humbly grow crops in his small patch and to look after a few cows. This man will construct his identity in a predominantly *relational* way, for he does not feel any power over the world nor can he even conceive of himself outside of the family he belongs to, the parish he lives in, or the mountains that enclose him. He will probably believe in the existence of God, or in other mythical beings, such as witches (or *meigas* in Galician) or dead who can reach out from the parallel spaces they inhabit and interact with us by virtue of their highly superior powers, taking away whoever crosses their path[4]. This man is part of the same society as the astrophysicist, but it would seem (as is in fact the case) that they live in different worlds. Between them lies an incredibly wide spectrum of individuation levels, which attest to the wide range of worlds inhabited by all other group members. This variety of possible worlds is correlative to the power differences that exist within the group.

Any individual person's level of individuation is nothing but the identity counterpart of their position of power/control/rational knowledge of the world, the cognitive correlate of that level of power. As has been explained, both dimensions contribute to develop each other, and they are two sides of the same coin: an increase in power causes an increase in individuation, but at the same time, the development of individuality (whether through learning to write or through a therapy that might lead someone to generate desires for themselves) implies an increased feeling of and capacity for power. And, conversely: a power loss will bring about an increase in relational identity to compensate for it and to restore confidence about one's own survival.

Identity is flexible; it can transform itself and will always operate as a cognitive resort to neutralize feelings of impotence. So, depending on the type of power relationship between someone and the world at any given moment, the mechanisms of either relational or individuated identity can be activated: possessing little power will activate relational identity; greater power will trigger individuated identity. Let us imagine a group of highly individuated people who, for reasons beyond their powers, are forced to face up to a new, unexpected threat: a war, a natural or nuclear disaster, an authoritarian ruler or tyranny, etc. As individuals under threat, they will automatically generate mechanisms of relational identity and unite in communities of struggle, resistance, or organization to allow themselves to believe in their chances of survival. At the same time, their identity will focus on the group which, among members of underground resistances, or those on opposing sides in wars, comes to act as a security-providing instance. Bonds with such groups are always of a mythical nature, and shared symbols are often endowed with a value just as sacred

---

[4] I am referring to the popular Galician belief in the *Santa Compaña*—The Holy Company—a procession of tormented souls who errantly wonder around country paths. Whoever catches a glimpse of them is drawn into the company. A brilliant analysis of the lethal character of encounters between the living and inhabitants of the mythical world among Amazonian groups can be found in Viveiros de Castro (1996: 135).

as that ascribed by hunter-gatherers to trees or mountains. In this case flags, party acronyms, or a wide variety of symbols represent that idealized abstract instance, allegiance to which is supposed to grant personal security. There is no space for any such thing as personal initiative if one wants to enjoy its protection, only for obedience and the humble accomplishment of the rites demanded by its sacred character and its protective powers. But if the state of threat should end and people go back to the specialized positions they once enjoyed within the group, then priority will be given again to the individuated identity they had enjoyed prior to the onset of the threat.

Similarly, multiple identities may overlap within a single person when subjected to oppression or exploitation on different levels: let us think, for example, of a black woman slave in a predominantly white patriarchal society. All three terms—woman, black, and slave—constitute subordinate conditions, so, as has been analyzed by other authors (Young 1983; Femenías 2008), people who embody these conditions will tend to construct collective identities of self-affirmation, that is, *relational* identities. It has been pointed out that where these *plural identities* exist, one of them will prevail over the others, depending on a wide number of different political factors, but I would dare to note that, as a rule, the prevailing relational identity—or the most visible one—will be the one linked to whichever relationship is experienced as generating the highest level of oppression or exploitation, the one experienced as the greatest threat. The greater the impotence, the stronger the relational identity. In the situation mentioned, for example, the most visible identity will probably be the one relating to the person's condition as a slave. But in the case of a nonslave black woman, she will identify more with either her race or her sex, depending on which one of them has caused her to endure greater levels of subordination throughout her life. For this reason most white middle-class women generally tend to contemplate only one level of relational identity, linked to gender, whereas feminists from other contexts perceive many more dimensions in domination, as well as their complex interrelations (Davis 1981; Mohanty et al. 1991). Not a single person's identity can possibly be understood without an assessment of their particular position in relation to the axes of power and domination that define their society. But this should not lead us to believe that there are no regularities when it comes to constructing personal identity, as claimed in postmodern quarters where some defend the absolute particularity of every subject and the impossibility of any comparison or generalization.[5] On the contrary, the only thing that this proves is that, if we are to understand the interplay of the two different sets of identity traits, we must take into account the particular historical and social context of each case, as these will always follow a similar logic in their relationship with power.

For these reasons, I reject any kind of evolutionist position in the humanities and social sciences. Individuated identity is no better than relational identity, nor can

---

[5] Postmodern feminist authors use the term *intersectionality* to refer to the crossroads of identities derived from race, class, and gender which, according to them, particularly defines each specific woman (Tanesini 1999; Brumfiel 2006). Analyses of this position can be read in Cobo (2011: 66) or in Lozano Rubio (2011).

judgment be passed on any of their endless possible combinations. All forms of identity are equally effective in constituting efficient means for people and groups to cope with their particular conditions of control over the world. *Contemporary society idealizes individuality and rejects relational identity because the former is associated with power and the latter to impotence.* But, as I hope to prove, the former is a sheer fantasy unless it relies on the latter, because a truly individual identity would merely expose any one person's sheer smallness and insufficiencies before the universe. To understand how this fantasy has been created and sustained, we must activate our archaeologist's gaze and focus on what patriarchal discourse hides yet is performed in the everyday lives of men, as part of that unconscious and *denied* level referred to above. We must focus our attention on the reality of things, not the discourse about that reality.

If we focus our attention closely on men with power's behavior, we will find that the process described above—by which, as the level of power/control over the world increased, relational identity was gradually substituted for individuated identity—actually took place only on the level of *appearances*. In fact, despite the rise of individual identity, relational identity never disappeared; it simply stopped being consciously acknowledged and began to be *denied*. As men developed their own individualities one step further, they began to perfom the same percentage of their relational identity unconsciously. Men's individuation process has, throughout history, been characterized by the unconscious performance of the same percentage of relational identity as it came to characterize their individuality. *Relational identity remains untouched in all human beings, because bonding with the group is fundamental to generating a sense of security.* It is only by relying on relational identity that individuality can be constructed to varying degrees, or not at all. If individuality is built up, people will embody within themselves two contradictory modes of identity in their relationship with the world. Far from acknowledging this contradiction, men have throughout history simply *denied* it, unconsciously performing that high percentage of relational identity and appearing to have supplemented it with individuality. This means that as their levels of individuation increased, so did the percentage of relational identity they performed unconsciously.

In order to *perform* that relational identity in an unconscious, and therefore *denied*, way, they used two mechanisms: (a) unequal gender relationships and (b) ascribed membership to peer groups, either within or outside of their own. My argument is that, historically, men have used both of these strategies to compensate, unwittingly and unrecognizably, the very deficits that individuality caused in their bonding and in their sense of belonging. Men have therefore erected their individuality upon a fantasy. Still, the discourse of truth sustaining the patriarchal order is so powerful that it can even render invisible what is in front of our very eyes. This way, we are brought up to believe that things are the way discourse tells us and not the way we can observe (without seeing) that they actually are. In the next two chapters, I will try to unravel the realm of this fantasized form of individuality in its full scope.

References

Bauman, Z. (2007). *Consuming life*. Cambridge/Malden: Polity Press.
Bird-David, N. (1999). 'Animism' revisited: Personhood, environment and relational epistemology. *Current Anthropology, 40*(Suppl), S67–S91.
Brumfiel, E. M. (2006). Methods in feminist and gender archaeology: A feeling for difference-likeness. In S. Milledge Nelson (Ed.), *Handbook of gender in archaeology* (pp. 30–58). Lanham: Altamira Press.
Cobo, R. (2011). *Hacia una nueva política sexual. Las mujeres ante la reacción patriarcal*. Catarata: Madrid.
Cohen, A. P. (1994). *Self-consciousness. An alternative anthropology of identity*. Londres: Routledge.
Davis, A. (1981). *Women, race and class*. Nueva York: Random House.
Dumont, L. (1986). *Essays on individualism: Modern ideology in anthropologial perspective*. Chicago: University of Chicago Press.
Ewing, K. P. (1990). The illusion of wholeness: Culture, self, and the experience of inconsistency. *Ethos, 18*(3), 251–278.
Femenías, M. L. (2008). Identidades esencializadas/violencias activadas. *Isegoría. Revista de Filosofía Moral y Política, 38*, 15–38.
Fowler, C. (2005). *The archaeology of personhood. An anthropological approach*. Londres: Routledge.
Fowler, C. H. (2016). Relational personhood revisited. *Cambridge Archaeological Journal, 26*(03), 397–412.
Geertz, C. (1984). From the native's point of view: On the nature of anthropological understanding. In R. A. Shweder & R. A. LeVine (Eds.), *Culture theory. Essays on mind, self, and emotion* (pp. 123–136). Cambridge: Cambridge University Press.
Hernando, A. (2000). Factores estructurales asociados a la identidad de género femenina. La no-inocencia de una construcción socio-cultural. In A. Hernando (Ed.), *La construcción de la subjetividad femenina* (pp. 101–142). Madrid: Instituto de Investigaciones Feministas.
Kashima, Y., Yamaguchi, S., Kim, U., Choi, S.-C., Gelfand, M. J., & Yuki, M. (1995). Culture, gender, and self: A perspective from individualism-collectivism research. *Journal of Personality and Social Psychology, 69*(5), 925–937.
Knapp, A. B., & Meskell, L. (1997). Bodies of evidence on prehistoric Cyprus. *Cambridge Archaeological Journal, 7*(2), 183–204.
Knapp, A. B., & Van Dommelen, P. (2008). Past practices: Rethinking individuals and agents in archaeology. *Cambridge Archaeological Journal, 18*(1), 15–34.
LiPuma, E. (2000). *Encompassing others. The magic of modernity in Melanesia*. Ann Arbor: University of Michigan Press.
Lozano Rubio, S. (2011). Gender thinking in the making. Feminist epistemology and gender archaeology. *Norwegian Archaeological Review, 44*(1), 21–39.
Machin, A. (2009). The role of the individual agent in Acheulean biface variability. *Journal of Social Archaeology, 9*(1), 35–58.
Markus, H. R., & Kitayama, S. (1991). Culture and the self: Implications for cognition, emotion and motivation. *Psychological Review, 98*(2), 224–253.
Mohanty, C. T., Russo, A., & Torres, L. (1991). *Third world women and the politics of feminism*. Bloomington/Indianápolis: Indiana University Press.
Moore, H. (2000). Ethics and ontology: Why agents and agency matter. In M. A. Dobres & J. E. Robb (Eds.), *Agency in archaeology* (pp. 259–263). Londres: Routledge.
Price-Williams, D. P. (1980). Anthropological approaches to cognition and their relevance to psychology. In H. C. Triandis & W. Lonner (Eds.), *Handbook of cross-cultural psychology. Basic processes* (Vol. 3, pp. 155–184). Boston: Allyn and Bacon.
Read, K. E. (1955). Morality and the concept of the person among the Gahuku-Gama. *Oceania, 25*, 233–282.

Sampson, E. E. (1988). The debate on individualism. Indigenous psychologies of the individual and their role in personal and societal functioning. *American Psychologist, 43*(1), 15–22.

Sennett, R. (1998). *The corrosion of character: The personal consequences of work in the new capitalism.* New York: Norton.

Shweder, R. A., & Bourne, E. J. (1982). Does the concept of the person vary cross-culturally? In A. J. Marsella & G. M. White (Eds.), *Cultural conceptions of mental health and therapy* (pp. 97–137). Dordrecht: Springer.

Sökefeld, M. (1999). Debating self, identity, and culture in anthropology. *Current Anthropology, 40*(4), 417–447.

Spiro, M. E. (1993). Is the western conception of the self 'peculiar' within the context of the world cultures? *Ethos, 21*(2), 107–153.

Strathern, M. (1988). *The gender of the gift. Problems with women and problems with society in Melanesia.* Berkeley: University of California Press.

Tanesini, A. (1999). *An introduction to feminist epistemologies.* Oxford: Blackwell.

Thomas, J. (2004). *Archaeology and modernity.* Londres: Routledge.

Virilio, P. (2005). *The Paul Virilio reader* (S. Redhead, Ed.). New York: Columbia University Press.

Viveiros de Castro, E. (1996). Os pronomes cosmológicos e o perspectivismo ameríndio. *Mana, 2*(2), 115–144.

Young, I. M. (1983). Is male gender identity the cause of male domination?. In J. Trabilcot (Comp.), *Mothering. essays in feminist theory* (pp. 129–143). Totowa: Rowman & Allenhed.

Chapter 7
The Fantasy of Individuality I: Women and Gender Identity

In this chapter, I would like to go back to the start of the process, where it all must have started, and to reassess and reveal the workings gradually concealed by the patriarchal order on its road to erecting its own power upon a fantasy. In so doing, I hope to contribute to two aims, which, disparate as they might appear, are in fact one and the same thing: to end the subordination of women and to transform the logic guiding our social order as it embarks on a seemingly accelerating drift toward an uncontrolled, hopeless, and painful future.

In order to approach the question of the subordination of women historically, I will begin by explaining the historical process suggested by the *official* account provided by prehistory manuals. Later, I will try to *complete* this reconstruction by analyzing the archaeological data available about women and the ways in which identity dynamics might have unfolded.

As has already been presented, a vast *corpus* of contemporary evidence proves how both men and women in groups without division of functions or work specialization carry out complementary tasks that do not necessarily imply power relations, as neither of them control or stand at an emotional distance from any of the phenomena that make up their lived reality nor, therefore, from any other group members. At the same time, however, it has also been proven that all known cases grant symbolic priority or greater prestige to the masculine, possibly resulting from the cognitive implications of the greater mobility inherent to those functions carried out by men. In the past, such a slightly greater mobility would also have been associated with an equally slightly greater assertiveness and ability to take decisions. As a result, the men would have found themselves in a better position to bring about small changes, geared not toward more profound transformations but rather toward maintaining the *status quo* in the inevitably changing conditions of interaction with the elements.

We could therefore assume that, having set out from a complementary but egalitarian relationship between the sexes and as the result of that almost imperceptible initial difference, men may have taken on a slightly greater responsibility in decision-making processes, slowly creating the conditions for inequality. Originally, this responsibility might not even have been taken up by isolated men—which would have implied power differences—but by groups of adult men, organized, for example, into such institutions as councils of the elderly. The archaeological record actually supports this type of process, which can be inferred, for example, from Andrew Sherratt's research (1982: figure 2.7) at two necropolises in the Balkans. The first, Nitra (in Slovakia), from the Late Neolithic period, dated at the start of the fifth millennium BC, shows men between 40 and 60 years of age buried with grave goods that set them apart from the rest of the group and strengthen their links with each other through the presence of polished stone axes and shell rings in all graves. This first period studied by Sherratt characteristically featured intensive agricultural production techniques, although specialized farming production was still lacking. Such farming practices only appeared in later phases, precisely those of the second necropolis. Dated at more than a thousand years later, in the fourth millennium BC, the Chalcolithic necropolis of Tiszapolgár-Basatanya (Hungary) includes grave goods illustrating different levels of wealth. This signals a clear development of inequality, both between the two sexes and among different members of them. The richest and most striking elements—daggers made of stone and copper (the first metal in the area)—were associated with "young adult males" (ibid.: 23), with variations in the presence of other grave goods from one individual to another. In the Chalcolithic, a division of functions already existed which went beyond that determined by sex, as proven not only by the start of specialized farming production to obtain *secondary products*—such as cheese, milk, or wool—but especially by the appearance of metallurgy and commercial networks. These socioeconomic traits are associated with the emergence of what are considered the first *chiefs* in the archaeological record, males identified by some with the figure of the "big man." Sahlins (1963) coined the term in Melanesia to identify men of authority and social recognition whose power was still not transmitted by inheritance. Such transmission, which would indicate strengthened positions of power by the legitimizing use of lineages, has been documented in the archaeological record in the Western world only from the Bronze Age on (at about 1.800 BC). It was at this moment that the first luxury grave goods appeared in the tombs of children, a case in point being the necropolises from the El Argar culture, in the Spanish southeast (Lull et al. 2004). These infants' tombs date back to the time of increased craft specialization when the earliest commercial networks were set up to obtain tin, which, alloyed with copper, could be used to make bronze. Ever since this moment, the socioeconomic process in what would later be known as the West, has become characterized, first, by a growing division of functions and technological specialization, associated with increasingly wide and complex relationship and exchange networks, conflicts, and alliances and, second, by the multiplication of positions of power and individuated identities.

Such is the account of prehistory manuals, which only take into account the development of technology, wealth, or those positions of power presumably held by men, all of which constitute mechanisms of emotional detachment from the world. The argument I have been repeating, however, is that, if such a detachment had indeed taken place, the sense of security generated by technological change would

7 The Fantasy of Individuality I: Women and Gender Identity

have been less compelling than the insecurity caused by these men's separation from the sacred instance and the group. The only possible way in which those changes could have taken place would be by retaining a sense of belonging to the group. I am absolutely persuaded of this, not only by the behaviors I presently observe in most men with power—whom we shall turn to below—but also by the very data provided by the historical and archaeological records. Let us then turn back now, to *complete* the picture of the identity process undergone by those men who acquired increasing power.

At the very start of all cultural trajectories, when all were hunter-gatherers, differences between men's and women's levels of individuation must have been practically nonexistent. Since both constructed their identities in relational ways, it would not be correct to describe those societies as patriarchal. At a later stage in the process, when men developed that minimal difference and slowly and subtly began to generate changes toward greater technological control, their loss of emotional connection was probably invisible and went unnoticed, for women would have compensated for it with their own slightly higher level of relational identity. However, this originally unplanned and undirected process began to gain momentum, and the initially imperceptible differences between men's and women's identities were to have transcendent consequences in all historical trajectories. As long as women compensated for men's loss of emotional connection, men could, in turn, raise their levels of technological control (i.e., of individuation) without even noticing their increased detachment and without relationships between men and women initially implying any sort of coercion or subordination. Relational identity and the protection granted by a sacred instance would continue to be perceived by the whole group as the main security mechanisms.

The situation would have become problematic when, through the constant reinforcing of these dynamics—with men remaining slightly more individuated and women retaining relational identity—the technological control, the level of power, and the individual features developed by men reached a level that created a conflict. At this point there was a clash between the importance that men themselves and the entire group gave to the security provided by each mechanism: on the one hand, protection from a sacred instance and on the other hand, technological control in the hands of men; in other words, between belonging to the group and individual agency. Because the former is paradoxically associated with insecurity, with weakness and with impotence before the world, whereas the latter is linked to self-confidence, initiative, and personal potency, it is logical to assume that, as men increasingly *specialized* in the latter, they found it harder and harder to recognize themselves in the former. We must bear in mind that, for each one of the phenomena they came to control, men gradually took on themselves the power they had formerly granted the sacred instance. The feeling of personal potency generated by this is in stark contrast to the powerlessness and humility inherent in perceiving oneself as a simple cog in the machine of one's own group. These are contradictory perceptions indeed: one associated with weakness, the other with strength; one with impotence, the other with power; one with submission to the powers of a protective instance, the other with agency and with personal initiative; one with the object position, the other with the subject position; and one with recurrence, the other with change. Also, and obviously, the ability to wield power over the world and to bring about changes multiplies when one perceives oneself as powerful, something for which *denying* insecurity is of great assistance. The problem lies in that, without keeping their links with the group, these men could not possibly have sustained their self-confidence, as the smallness of their own power before the universe would have become evident to them... It seems an unsolvable problem, but in fact it was not. *Denying* the contradiction, at the price of, among other strategies, women's subordination, embodied the solution.

From the entire process outlined, it can be safely inferred that while the fraction of phenomena which could be controlled/explained rationally remained low, so did both men's degree of individuation and the power differences associated with gender relationships. However, as these dynamics began to generate changes and men's individuality and power grew, the contradiction also became more flagrant. The more importance given to rational distance as the basis of power, the more value would be taken away from the conscious, public, and social recognition of the fact that group belonging was indispensable to sustain it, just as important as it had ever been, and to the exact same extent. This was how, in a very gradual and almost imperceptible way at the start of the process, the *system* was able to function in a way that put women in charge of the (socially unrecognized) task of guaranteeing sustained bonds for men who, while becoming increasingly unable to cultivate these, could not possibly live without them. This would have required a compulsory heterosexuality— to grant complementarity to these *specializations*, at the same time that it would have boost differences between both forms of identity and power, as men's levels of individuation, rationalization, and technological control continued to rise. At a certain point in this process, it became vital for men that women should maintain their *relational identity* as reliable sources of the very bonds and sense of belonging whose social importance they themselves recognized less and less, what signals the onset of the patriarchal order. Men would have needed this emotional *assistance* so strongly that they could not possibly allow women to become individuated. If that ever happened, the potency fantasy that men lived in would become evident to them, as would the basic impotence and the essential and transcendental insecurity that lies at the core of all human beings' relationship with the world. If this had happened, men would be confronted with the truth that their discourse *denies*. It was at this very point that the domination over women, which is associated with patriarchal order, began. For these reasons, I call the form of identity developed by men throughout history *dependent individuality*, for it cannot be constructed without leaning on another person's specialized emotional support, which is the role historically played by women. I thus also contend that the key to its construction and to the ensuing social discourse lies in the *dissociation of reason from emotion* and in the *denial of the importance of emotions* for the survival of groups, in the *fantasy of individuality*.

In turn, women would have kept contributing to function complementarity by maintaining relational identity and by entrusting men—gradually and to the extent that they were able to control natural phenomena—with the functions of group

7 The Fantasy of Individuality I: Women and Gender Identity

Fig. 7.1 "Female gender identity" as relational identity

No specialized functions
Recurrent (domestic) activities
Personal logic is attributed to all external phenomena: the person is the center of their own world
Emotional relationship (as well as non-abstract rational) with all the elements of reality
FEMALE GENDER IDENTITY (RELATIONAL)
Change is assessed in a negative way, because it implies risk
(Domestic) space constitutes the most visible axis for organizing reality
FEELS POWERLESS BEFORE THE WORLD
Trust in destiny and survival is placed in *a man* with whom a dependent and subordinate relationship is established
Security is based on the confidence of having been chosen by *a man* : OBJECT position
No desires are generated for oneself, and, instead, there is a permanent preoccupation to identify and satisfy those of the *man* who provides security

protectors and *subjects*, which they had so far only attributed to the sacred instance. So, while God would initially have been considered the only protective instance, at a later stage, both God and men with power began to be perceived as sources of security and protection by those—the rest of the men and all of the women—who retained their relational identity within the group. And so, as the division of functions intensified, and all the men developed some degree of individuation, *pure* relational identity was relegated to women, who kept the same subordinate position toward God as they did toward men. For this very reason, it is my opinion that what we presently identify as *female gender identity* is nothing but the same type of *relational identity* as we have described for both the men and women of hunter-gatherer groups.

In fact, if, in the *relational identity* chart shown in Fig. 4.1, we substitute the term *sacred instance* for the term *man*, as I have done in Fig. 7.1, my point will become clear: until the arrival of modernity, women typically developed (and continue to do so in any society where functional division does not coincide with that of the Western world) nonspecialized and recurrent tasks, such as home care and group reproduction (or agricultural activities when they participate in tasks external to the household). These are always carried out in familiar (domestic) spaces, which are as emotionally charged as nature used to be for hunter-gatherers. For this very reason, space has priority over time as an ordering parameter, for the latter does not organize changes and is therefore not perceived in a linear way, with different pasts, presents, and futures, but cyclically (as will be clear to anyone who has looked after a household). These women's identities are constructed through the relationships they establish and keep and not through their individual selves, so belonging to family networks (regardless of type) becomes indispensable. In fact, being excluded from these (as proven by many cases of abused women) can sometimes take a much greater and more distressing toll than the suffering caused by the relationships themselves, as was the case with the Txukahamei (see Chap. 4). Finally, women who represent this type of identity do not generate any desires for themselves, as their security depends on recognizing and satisfying those of the man who provides that security (along with those of God). As among hunter-gatherers, the impotence inherent to this type of identity is compensated for by a perception of themselves at the center of all the emotional dynamics surrounding them: if these women's boss, husband, or friend should ever be angry at them, they will dwell endlessly on every single detail and on the possible injustice of the case, instead of considering the annoyance to have possibly been caused by their boss/husband/friend's own difficulties, problems, or tensions outside of the relationship they have with them. Absolutely everything that happens is explained in terms of personal relationships, charging up life itself with emotions, magnifying one's own importance in the universe, and compensating for the insecurity felt before it.[1]

Women with this type of identity may even feel a certain sense of power that can cause them to *deny* their own subordinate position. Since men invest more energy and consciousness in their rational relationship with the world, the set of repressed emotions that comes to constitute their *self* becomes a hidden world, unbeknownst to themselves, one that they can cope with all the worse the more they get to know and manage the reasons that explain the outside world. Therefore, the greater the security these men feel in managing reasons, the greater the insecurity that invades them when it comes to coping with emotions; the more they come to control the outside world, the less they can handle their own inner worlds that women have precisely and slowly been made to specialize in. This also explains why some women in contexts of highly unequal gender relationships can feel great power within the family. For, within its realm, they can carry out the indispensable role of making the man feel secure and the family function. Such a power, however, is very different from that inherent to individuality: while the latter is based on the objectification of other human beings, the power of relational identity is based on the implicit or explicit knowledge of their subjectivities; while the power of individuality can be exerted over an undefined number of strangers, the power of relational identity can only be exerted over someone with whom a relationship of dependence already exists; while the former affects the destinies of the whole group, the latter

---

[1] Levinton (2000) analyzes, from a feminist psychoanalytic perspective, the *norms* and *ideals* of what she calls the feminine *gender format*.

only affects that of the husband and children, who might even feel (as is sometimes voiced by men of rigid patriarchal mentality) that, underneath it all "it is the women who are in charge," when in fact social evidence points to the exact opposite.

It must also be taken into consideration that a gender relationship where one part has *dependent individuality* and the other *relational identity* is always a power relationship based on complementarity, so each one of its members is essential to the other. For this reason, the power relationship it implies might possibly go unnoticed when and if it is built on affection and personal respect. In this sense, when I state that men gradually took away the value and recognition from the function fulfilled by women, I am referring to social not personal value: (patriarchal) social discourse does not acknowledge the fundamental importance of this function for the group's survival and sense of security, but each individual man may recognize their wife's contribution to their own personal welfare. It may happen that contempt or social undervaluing should become intertwined with personal feelings, therefore leading to aggressiveness and violence, but this is not inherent to the relationship itself. In fact, I believe it is precisely because *gender inequality* and *gender violence* are often equated that many men who would never resort to the latter fail to recognize the power relationship that sustains their own sentimental lives.

In any case, historically men slowly came to *delegate*—today we might say that they *outsourced*—their capacity to feel linked with the group to women. And they became more and more dependent on these women the more importance they themselves granted to reason as a reassurance mechanism. This was in itself a contradiction, as the less men recognized women's function and contribution to group survival, the more they depended on them. I would even say that it was men's very perception of their own dependence that generated rejection toward the function fulfilled by the women they needed so badly. Women and their function revealed the very impotence that they had put so much effort into denying. The intense misogyny that accompanied the emergence of writing in ancient Greece is a case in point, as it had been absent from the—predominantly oral—period that went before it, Archaic Greece (Madrid 1999; Pomeroy 1999). As these men started to engage in the world through abstract thought, their levels of individuation rocketed, and so did gender inequality and men's contempt toward everything represented by the function fulfilled by women. Those very needs were more undervalued and denied the more conspicuous they became, and, therefore, so was the function carried out by women.

It must be highlighted again that the entire process must have been unconscious and unplanned and that it gradually and imperceptibly developed through the changing socialization of group members. As socioeconomic complexity increased, so did differences in the level of individuation of normative gender models: men would increasingly be rewarded for using reason and for repressing their emotions, while women were encouraged to do the opposite. At the same time, heterosexuality became more strictly enforced the more dissociated men's identity grew and the more they relied on women's *relational* identity. Socialized in this complementarity, all group members would slowly transmit a differentiated model to their sons and daughters, further widening the gap between the respective identities that boys and girls were to develop as adults. This was probably also shaped biologically by the gradual differentiation of the type of synapses and neuronal connections they would develop throughout their upbringing and education.

As I have pointed out, I do not think that historical attempts to render women invisible have originated in their sex but in the fact that they came to specialize in sustaining bonds and emotional connection. The importance of both was gradually *denied* by men who increasingly heralded reason and technology as the sole foundations of their power. For this reason, when it comes to accounting for the transformations that define our own trajectory, science and history—the basis of our social and legitimizing discourses—recognize only those dynamics that are connected to reason, and not the ones connected to emotion. In this light, it hardly comes as a surprise that the academic and scientific world remains resistant to feminist or gender studies, consistently prevented by all imaginable means from integrating its central corpus of knowledge. I state that this hardly comes as a surprise because feminist studies are proving everything that the entire discourse of *truth* guiding our own social order had so far denied: the repression unleashed against the individuation of women when some of them, because they belonged to elite groups or families, learned to read and write; the fundamental contribution made to group support by those who retained relational identity,[2] and the complexity, the power struggles, and the exercise of domination over women that defines the entire historical process.

And yet, the academic world also includes those (especially women, of course) who construct their own identities along lines different from *dependent individuality* and who, because of the same *fractal* relationship referred to in Chap. 1, are able to see through the deceptions of social discourse (e.g., Morant 2005). I must stress that this accomplishment requires a subjective effort that is hard to explain to anyone who has never attempted it, as the (dissociated) logical order that rules our own society requires the insistent reinforcement of certain worldviews. Overcoming these and learning to build new relationships represent a demanding fresh start with one's own subjectivity, which only those readers who have attempted it personally will be able even to conceive of, as through our upbringing we are taught to *look* at the world in a certain way that we consider to be the *only* possible one, when it is in fact a construct built on the *denials* of those who sustain power within our social order, a by-product of the set of denials that constitute the building blocks of an established but alleged *truth*. Therefore, by the same token, as soon as we deactivate the *denials* upon which this discourse and power rest, everything that had been there but remained unseen and concealed by discourse is uncovered before our eyes.

Without developing a full historical reconstruction, which would be beyond the scope of this book, I would like to present some data that illustrate how threatening men must have found the possibility that women might become individuated. The reason was that, if women were to abandon their relational identity, this would undo

---

[2] A new trend in archaeology is devoted to rescuing the value of the so-called maintenance activities, (i.e., group care and maintenance) carried out by women over the centuries and neglected by traditional archaeology (Montón-Subías and Sánchez-Romero 2008 [eds.]).

the *fantasy of individuality* sustaining men's own power. That portion of history, which does not appear in textbooks, shows the extent to which *relational or gender identity* is not a function of any essence or biological imperatives. On the contrary, it stems from the very social dynamics that forced women into a single model of identity, which included mechanisms of punishment and exclusion for those of them who dared to abandon it.

7.1 The Repression of Women's Mobility and Writing

I have put forward the argument that, in oral societies, mobility is structurally associated with individuality: the greater people's mobility, the more they need to face up to several types of different phenomena, to make decisions, and to behave assertively. Because these are not causal but structural relationships, the opposite will also hold true, that is, that the more individuated people are, the greater capacity and desire they will have to transit different spaces, due to their greater capacity to face up to the unknown. For this reason, limitations on mobility are powerful strategies for containing individuality and the power associated with it (remember the phrase that a woman should be "barefoot and pregnant in the kitchen," where the bare feet emphasize the limits that should be imposed on a good wife's mobility outside of the home). As has also been explained above, writing constitutes a powerful tool of individuation, for representing the world's dynamics through abstract models is tantamount to understanding them, and that generates a feeling of power over them. In this way, in literate societies, barring women from learning to read and write has been a formidable tool against their individuation. Both these strategies have been used against women.

As we have seen, throughout the history of the Western world, it was only toward the Final Neolithic/Chalcolithic/Early Bronze Age that differentiated positions of power emerged. At that time a set of innovations were introduced from the Near East and the Eastern European steppes that allowed the farming of soils of much poorer quality, and hence a significant rise in production, transforming socioeconomic organization in a way that lead Andrew Sherratt (1981, 1986) to coin the term "secondary products revolution." Among the main innovations were the plough, the ox, the horse, and the cart, which allowed populations to occupy hitherto unarable land and lead to an increase in the mobility and transport of both people and products, in turn boosting commerce and intragroup functional diversification. These innovations permitted, among other things, the use of vacant lands for grazing cattle, as is documented by pollen analyses which indicate the advance of deforestation, and the start of flint mining to make stone axes. Specialized farming production thus began to yield secondary products such as milk and wool to make cheese and clothes, as indicated by the archaeological remains related with these activities. Researchers of this process (Sherratt 1981: 297; Robb 1994: 36; Randsborg 1984: 148) have also traced a transformation in the economic functions fulfilled by each sex. Grave goods suggest that men came to specialize in such tasks as herding and commerce, while women would have taken up other responsibilities, such as weaving and making cheese, which were more easily compatible with looking after their increasingly numerous offspring—agriculture boosted demographic growth, as the new value of children as a useful workforce for the domestic unit eliminated the previous need to contain infant population levels. Note the implications of each type of activity on the mobility of each sex: herding and commerce caused an increase in the mobility required of men by the agricultural tasks they had hitherto undertaken, while the production of wool, cheese, and woven cloth (the *secondary products*) meant a relative reduction of women's mobility. In my opinion, that moment of our historical trajectory—around 2500 BC—could be aptly described as the start of the *patriarchal order*.

In fact, at the start of this process, the archaeological record not only reflects the emergence of the earliest *chiefs* (which shall be described in further detail in the next chapter) but it also proves that in the Bronze Age, toward 1500 BC, identity differences between men and women were already a part of the social *norm* (Hernando 2005). In certain central and northern European contexts, where preservation conditions have allowed archaeologists to scrutinize dress, they have ascertained the existence of *regional dresses*, also known as "identity dresses" (Wels-Weyrauch 1994), which, as among hunter-gatherers, differentiate communities. It has also been observed how, unlike hunter-gatherer groups, those Bronze-Age communities featured a single type of dress for the men, whereas there were two types for women: some wore a short skirt and no headdress in their hair, while others wore a long skirt and headdress, as shown, for example, in a German case; or some women wore metallic ornaments that highlighted their shoulders, and others wore the same type of ornament to highlight their hips, as in another Danish case (ibid.; Sørensen 1991: 125–127, 2000: 138). Since this double dress has no connection with either age or the season in which the women died (Sørensen 2000: 137), archaeologist Marie Louise Sørensen concludes that in the Bronze Age, men already represented a self-sustaining category, while the two existing categories of women were defined in relation to him, that is, through their social or marital status (Sørensen 1991: 127).

I would like also to add a piece of information about this moment, which, though seemingly anecdotal, is particularly striking. Among the several bronze ornaments worn by these women, a particular one is typically found in certain Central European areas: a double metal clamp worn around the shins, which are joined together by a metallic chain. The clamp is fastened, and the chain can be used to either hold together or release the shins alternatively or even to hold the shins together on a permanent basis (Sørensen 1997: 108 and figure 6; Wels-Weyrauch 1994: figure 56c). This *ornament* would probably be a status symbol, as the raw material it is made of (bronze) is highly valued, demanded, and often beautifully decorated. But it would also impose obvious limits on women's mobility, forcing them to walk and move in a way that one cannot but associate with the effect of the bandaging of the feet that used to cause the feet of Chinese women of privileged status to atrophy. To the extent that they almost prevent mobility altogether, both the clamp and the bandaging (covered by tiny shoes) impose severe restrictions on movement.

7.1 The Repression of Women's Mobility and Writing

It must be remembered that once power differences had become one of a group's traits, women born into more powerful families or lineages would have been socialized into a perception of themselves as having certain power and distance from women (or even men) of lower social strata. This meant that these women's identities would include certain individuating features, which would be enhanced or neutralized to suit the interests of their own lineages. Consider all the queens and women rulers in history, who have all too often been attributed *masculinized* identities, but who were simply highly individuated. Another good case in point was women in the classic world (Hellenistic and Roman) who, as part of their elite training, were taught to write. The Etruscan case is particularly unknown, for the Etruscans were assimilated into the rigidly patriarchal Roman order, causing their practices to fall into almost complete oblivion. Although Etruscan aristocratic women did not—under the patriarchal Etruscan system—participate in political power, they did, however, have a much more egalitarian relationship with men than in any other Mediterranean society. Indeed, significantly, Etruscan funerary grave goods feature pottery with written signs, alongside some horse bit mouthpieces and carts (Marín Aguilera 2016: 269, 273–4), all symbols of mobility. In turn, in the final stages of the Roman Republic and the Roman Empire, women of the elite were also allowed to learn to write, as befitted by the development of a separate identity from that of the rest of the social group, which was associated with family power. This training was explicitly justified as a way of enabling them to manage household expenses (Martínez 2005: 166). However, while obviously individuated and *empowered* by writing, young Roman women (as opposed to young men) could not leave the house to study, which effectively prevented them from training with philosophers or rhetoricians (Pomeroy 1999: 193), in addition to hampering their training in abstract thought. Once again, society limited their mobility.

Throughout history, socialization processes that instilled an awareness of one's distinction and belonging to elite groups have included writing, precisely because its individuating effect builds that feeling of distinction, of difference. However, while men were allowed to turn to society to fully realize its more creative and agentic possibilities, in the case of women, writing ran counter to the functions available to them within the patriarchal order, which required their sheer *relational identity*. The higher their social position or the more educated the family they belonged to, the more flagrant the contradictions they had to face. Highly individuated as their identities might be, they were not allowed to develop these within society. But then, how to realize it? Only on the margins of society could they be who they wanted to be.

Excluded from universities ever since these were created in the eleventh century, women who did not adapt to the norm of relational or gender identity could find a space for life and personal expression only in religious contexts and on condition that they renounced their own reproduction, both biological and social. Ángela Muñoz (1999, 2001, 2005, 2008), who has closely studied the relationships between women and religious institutions in the Iberian Peninsula in the middle ages, provides interesting information. Muñoz analyzes, for example, the many movements of "active celibates," which, existing since the earliest ages, later multiplied into an enormous diversity of social forms (friaresses, Hospitalleresses, *sorores*, priestesses, female hermits, luminaries, devotees, Beguines, secluded nuns, tertiaries, walled-in women, holy women/*beatae*) who characterized themselves either by engaging very actively in relief aid in urban contexts (including teaching young girls to write) or by secluding themselves as hermits or eremites, altogether fleeing society. The phenomenon was so widespread between the twelfth and sixteenth centuries, correlatively to the multiplication of social functions and the increase of masculine individuation, that it has been called the "feminine religious movement." These were lay organizations, outside of the norms of established ecclesiastical institutions and jurisdictions, which had no formulae of perpetual vows, enabling their members to change their lifestyle whenever they so wished. The contacts they kept among themselves, through letters and trips (that is, through writing and mobility), became international (Rivera 2005: 752), and their social visibility was such that in the sixteenth, seventeenth, and eighteenth centuries they were listed by the Inquisition as "deviant conducts," inquisitorial courts eventually putting an end to their very existence (Muñoz 2001:62).

Although this form signaled the greatest liberty and autonomy enjoyed by women in premodern Europe, early Christian monasteries also constituted a space for them to develop a more individuated identity than they were ever allowed in society at large (given the association between Christianity and writing, which we will not develop here), which explains so many queens', noblewomen's, and princesses' keenness to profess and to found. Muñoz shows how women turned convents into spaces of culture, creation, and interaction outside of marital submission both for nuns themselves and for the rest of society. Increasing demand for these places, however, led the Catholic church to obstruct this expression of female individuation, and in the early thirteenth century the Fourth Lateran Council forbade the creation of new female religious orders (Muñoz 2008) and placed all preexisting ones under the authority of masculine orders (Orlandis 1971: 20). And yet, institutional submission was not enough.

The very existence of these spaces of greater freedom for women was threatening enough in itself, and, as Muñoz goes on to argue, although they could not altogether be banned from a society which was guided by the very values these spaces represented, severe strategies of concealment were put to use. In 1298, Pope Boniface VII established the norm of seclusion which would henceforth characterize women's convents, as opposed to men's. Through this norm the mobility of nuns and abbotesses was irreversibly curtailed, and they were definitively isolated and confined away from society.

Despite these efforts, women continued to arrive at convents in great numbers, and the norm was relaxed, allowing lively and increasing interactions between religious and lay women. The latter were able to spend long periods of time at a convent or even move in with their servants and wealth on a permanent basis. But such disruptive behavior was definitively eradicated in 1493. This happened one year after the so-called "discovery" of America, at a time when the Western world's commercial networks were multiplying along with its social functions and technologies.

7.1 The Repression of Women's Mobility and Writing

The newly invented printing press allowed texts and readers to proliferate, and the individuation and power of its male members was increasingly shaping Western society. Between 1545 and 1563, the Council of Trent laid down draconian regulations about feminine seclusion, especially by defining the "strict praxis of spatial limits" (Muñoz 2005: 740). Walls were erected, windows and doors reduced, and the intense social interaction that had so far characterized women's convents was met with the obligation to build window grilles (never a feature of male convents) to definitively seclude and control those who had dared to challenge the social norm. Significantly, some reformers added a seemingly minor norm: "Nuns shall not be allowed to receive letters or to write them" (ibid.: 741). Mobility and writing. Writing and mobility.

This way, a thick layer of cement gradually came to cover all the cracks through which some women had managed to escape the tight gender norm of the only social building they had been allowed to inhabit. Even so, the irrepressible individuality of women from privileged groups or of those who could read and write continued to leak through the pores of the social body, seeking exits, means of expression, and every possibility of existence. Those who dared to experiment within their own society would soon learn that they might even be made to pay the price for their transgressions with their lives. They were identified with the devil, considered the root of all evil, accused of witchcraft, and tortured to death (Beteta 2011). Spaces of internment continued to be the only escape route. Secluded behind solid monastic walls, detached from any social links, they still found more freedom in that form of captivity than in marriage. In fact, one might argue that the very social immobility and isolation that were forced upon them created the conditions for them to express the type of "outside-the-world" individuality (of *outworldly* individuals) that Dumont has described among Indian ascetics in India and that constitutes the mystical path. As opposed to the "in-the world" individuality developed in the West (one of *inwardly* individuals), the individuality associated with mystique requires the persons to detach themselves from society and its reproduction. Such an identity creates a perception of oneself that clearly differentiating the person from the rest fills the individual with a certain potency, a potency that, in contrast to the one characterizing men in the Western world, is not attained through distancing oneself from the sacred but rather through achieving emotional fusion with it. Although persons who embody it may *feel* power, and their social authority may be recognized (as is the case with shamans, another form of individuation in more egalitarian societies), these individuals lack any formal political power and cannot rule over any other person's destiny. These forms of individuality are associated with neither work specialization nor technological control but with absolute subordination before the sacred instance which is the sole foundation of the power they feel. Since this type of identity only redoubled the already subordinate position of women and required their detachment from social dynamics, it was the only form of individuality officially available to women until modernity.

Let us continue revising more historical data. As has been stated above, power in any given society is necessarily associated with the discourses of truth underpinning it. This means that in order to be effective, social practices have to be sustained by a clear discourse of social legitimation. From this perspective, some of the changes undergone by the mythical discourse upholding European (patriarchal) society are truly telling: the cult of the Virgin Mary, for example, became widespread in parallel with the trends toward individuation, functional division, and the increase of commerce from the eleventh and twelfth centuries (Warner 2013; Muñoz 1999: 86; Rougemont 1956). This was, without the slightest nuance, the most blatant model ever proposed of a woman with a purely *relational identity*, without any desires of her own (significantly, especially not sexual desires), whose only aspiration was maternity, which was to be enshrined forever as the ideal aspiration for all women. It will therefore come as no surprise that in 1854, when industrialization and modernity had begun to require women's specialization and consequently encouraged them to individuate, the immaculate conception (without original sin) of Mary (associated with her own virginity when she conceived Jesus Christ) became dogma (Warner 2013; Muñoz 1999: 82). That is, the absolute absence of desire for oneself was reinforced as the main attribute of the ideal female model.

If myth left no doubts whatsoever about the social models it espoused, science—the other legitimizing discourse which slowly came to replace it—made little room for speculation. At a time of transition between both legitimizing discourses, science had not yet secured a position from which to banish myth altogether. In fact, science continued to seek its own connections with myth as a way of eventually replacing it in the privileged sun of social discourse when Carl Linnaeus published his *Systema Naturae* (1735[3]). Linnaeus was a creationist whose intention was to prove God's supreme wisdom and goodness by revealing the plan He had followed in creation. In order to do so, Linnaeus invented a brand new classification system, which operated according to living beings' reproduction systems and which turned out so useful that it was later taken up by Darwin as a taxonomy for his own theory of evolution. Linnaeus skillfully based himself on myth while providing science with one of the main resources to sustain patriarchal order. He invented the notion of *species*, classifying living beings into five categories that were to multiply over the years: kingdom, class, order, genus, and species. Each species' designation was made up of two names, the genus and the species, which had to be grammatically consistent. Our own species was classified into the following categories: kingdom, Animalia; class, Mammalia; order, Primates; genus, *Homo*; and species, *sapiens*. Our biological name is therefore *Homo sapiens*, "knowing man." Linnaeus thereby lent scientific standing to the pretense that reason is an attribute of men, and not of women. Through abstract scientific classifications, he reformulated the basic belief underlying the myth: that the creator, who knows and names, is man. Woman was (and should only be) a mother without desires of her own. Notice that Linnaeus slyly picked an exclusively female trait, breasts, related to maternity, to connect our species with the rest of animals (Mammalia, mammals), while choosing the male's name, *Homo*, man, to set it apart from all other animals and grant it singularity

---

[3] Although this is the tenth edition, published in 1758, it is considered the canonical one.

(Schiebinger 1996: 144). Linnaeus chose a female trait related to maternity (ibid.: 138) to signal what our species has in common with others, such as sheep, dogs, or cows. And he chose what he considered to be men's *own* feature—reason—to mark the difference between our biological group and the rest. The hidden logical trap locked into the entire reasoning is perhaps better understood if we notice that out of the five classes Linnaeus used to divide animals (Mammalia, Amphibia, Pisces, Insecta, and Vermes), he only used the differentiating traits between males and females to group our species with other animals. While, obviously, women *do* have breasts, the point is that he could have classified our species by any other criterion, such as breathing system, way of feeding, etc., without emphasizing the difference between the sexes, as he did in all other classifications. The more unconscious the basis of a certain logic, the more penetrating it becomes, because the less resistance is opposed to it. And thus, science took up the baton from myth in this endless and ever-present effort, built layer upon layer upon layer upon layer of meanings, endlessly and invariably aimed at making women reinforce a subjectivity where they will not feel legitimated to (nor, in general, desire to) take on social roles related to reason, individuality, or power (see also Querol and Treviño 2005).

With the arrival of modernity, however, the very dynamics of increasing division of functions began to favor women's specialization. The crucial point was that when and if women were allowed to carry out as specialized tasks as men, they would become just as individuated, as was in fact the case. This broke the linearity of a logic that had so far guided the entire social process and faced the system with a contradiction which it has yet to solve: if women are allowed to become individuated, men lose a support that is indispensable to them, but if they are not, the system will not possibly be able to continue with its exponential growth. And this inconsistency charges the patriarchal order with a level of contradiction that causes its future trajectory to become utterly unpredictable from the point of view of identity.

And yet, before analyzing this, we should review another mechanism that men have used to construct the *fantasy of individuality*; one that, although as evident as the subordination of women, is equally invisible for those who see the world through the thick veil of the patriarchal order.

References

Beteta, Y. (2011). *Súcubos, hechiceras y monstruos femeninos. Estrategias de desautorización femenina en la ficción bajomedieval*. Madrid: Almudayna.
de Rougemont, D. (1956). *Love in the Western world*. Princeton: University Press.
Hernando, A. (2005). Agricultoras y campesinas en las primeras sociedades productoras. In Isabel Morant (Dir.), *Historia de las mujeres en España y América Latina* (Vol. I, pp. 79–115). Madrid: Cátedra.
Levinton, N. (2000). Normas e ideales del formato de género. In A. Hernando (Coord.), *La construcción de la subjetividad femenina* (pp. 53–99). Madrid: Instituto de Investigaciones Feministas.

Lull, V., Rihuete, C., Micó, R., & Risch, R. (2004). Las relaciones de propiedad en la sociedad argárica. Una aproximación a través del análisis de las tumbas de individuos infantiles. *Mainake, 26*, 233–272.
Madrid, M. (1999). *La misoginia en Grecia*. Madrid: Cátedra.
Marín Aguilera, B. (2016). Bajo la mirada clásica: la posición social femenina como amenaza para el poder masculino. In A. Bar-Magen, M. Crespo, A. Daza, M. Lanz (Eds.), *V Jornadas de Investigación del Departamento de Prehistoria y Arqueología de la UAM*, 6–8 de abril de 2011. Madrid: UAM Ediciones/Colección Actas CD.
Martínez, C. (2005). Los espacios de las mujeres hispanas. In I. Morant (Dir.), *Historia de las mujeres en España y América Latina* (Vol. I, pp. 153–192). Madrid: Cátedra.
Montón-Subías, S., & Sánchez-Romero, M. (Eds.). (2008). *Engendering social dynamics. The archaeology of maintenance activities*, British Archaeological Reports, Archaeological Series 1862. Oxford: Archaeopress.
Morant, I. (Dir.) (2005). *Historia de las mujeres en España y América Latina*. Madrid: Cátedra.
Muñoz, Á. (1999). El monacato como espacio de cultura femenina. A propósito de la Inmaculada Concepción de María y la representación de la sexuación femenina. In M. Nash, M. J. de la Pascua, & G. Espigado (Eds.), *Pautas históricas de sociabilidad femenina. Rituales y modelos de representación* (pp. 71–89). Cádiz: Servicio de Publicaciones de la Universidad de Cádiz.
Muñoz, Á. (2001, February). Fent món en el món. El moviment religiós femení castellà. Segles XII–XVI. *L'Avenç*, Dossier *Dones i monaquisme. Vida Religiosa:* 60–65.
Muñoz, Á. (2005). Mujeres y religión en las sociedades ibéricas: voces y espacios, ecos y confines (siglos XIII–XVI). In I. Morant (Dir.), *Historia de las mujeres en España y América Latina* (Vol. I, pp. 713–743). Madrid: Cátedra.
Muñoz, Á. (2008). Ser monja en la Edad Media. La disciplina e indisciplina del hábito. In *La Historia no contada. Mujeres pioneras* (pp. 29–43). Albacete: Editora Municipal.
Orlandis, J. (1971). *Estudios sobre instituciones monásticas medievales*. Pamplona: Ediciones de la Universidad de Navarra.
Pomeroy, S. B. (1999). *Diosas, rameras, esposas y esclavas. Mujeres en la Antigüedad Clásica*. Akal: Madrid.
Querol, M. Á., & Treviño, C. (2005). *La mujer en el origen del hombre*. Barcelona: Bellaterra.
Randsborg, K. (1984). Women in prehistory: The Danish example. *Acta Archaeologica, 55*, 143–154.
Rivera, M. M. (2005). Las beguinas y beatas, las trovadoras y las cátaras: el sentido libre del ser mujer. In Isabel Morant (Dir.), *Historia de las mujeres en España y América Latina* (Vol. I, pp. 745–767). Madrid: Cátedra.
Robb, J. (1994). Gender contradictions, moral coalitions, and inequality in Prehistoric Italy. *Journal of European Archaeology, 2*(1), 20–49.
Sahlins, M. (1963). Poor man, rich man, big man, chief: Political types in Melanesia and Polynesia. *Comparative Studies in Society and History, 5*, 285–303.
Schiebinger, L. (1996). Why mammals are called mammals: Gender politics in Eighteenth-Century natural history. In E. Fox Keller & H. E. Longino (Eds.), *Feminism and science* (pp. 137–153). Oxford: Oxford University Press.
Sherratt, A. (1981). Plough and pastoralism: Aspects of the secondary products revolution. In I. Hodder, G. Isaac, & N. Hammond (Eds.), *Pattern of the past. Studies in honour of David Clarke* (pp. 261–303). Cambridge: Cambridge University Press.
Sherratt, A. (1982). Mobile resources: settlement and exchange in early agricultural Europe. In C. Renfrew & S. Shennan (Eds.), *Ranking, resource and exchange. Aspects of the archaeology of early European society* (pp. 13–26). Cambridge: Cambridge University Press.
Sherratt, A. (1986). Wool, wheels and plughmarks: Local developments or outside introductions in Neolithic Europe? *Institute of Archaeology Bulletin, 23*, 1–15.

Sørensen, M. L. S. (1991). The Construction of gender through appearance. In D. Walde & N. D. Willows (Eds.), *The archaeology of gender*. Proceedings of the 22nd annual conference of the Archaeological Association of the University of Calgary (pp. 121–129). Calgary: The University of Calgary Press.

Sørensen, M. L. S. (1997). Reading dress: The construction of social categories and identities in Bronze Age Europe. *Journal of European Archaeology, 5*(1), 93–114.

Sørensen, M. L. S. (2000). *Gender Archaeology*. Cambridge: Polity Press.

Warner, M. (2013) [1976]. *Alone of all her sex: The myth and cult of the Virgin Mary*. Oxford: Oxford University Press.

Wels-Weyrauch, U. (1994). In Grab enhalten, im Leben Getragen – Tracht und Schmuck der Frau. In A. Jockenhövel & W. Kubach (Eds.), *Bronzezeit in Dutschland* (pp. 59–64). Stuttgart: Theiss.

Chapter 8
The Fantasy of Individuality II: Men's (Unconscious) Performance of Relational Identity

Emotional connection with one's group is an indispensable part of all human identities. In fact, it is so important that its *outsourcing* through gender relations is insufficient for persons with *dependent individuality,* who will also perform their own connection through unconscious mechanisms that remain unacknowledged by social discourse. The present chapter is devoted to proving this point.

As has been presented when analyzing *relational identity*, ascription to groups can be conveyed by a common appearance: Awá or Q'eqchi's, for example, are not Awá or Q'eqchi's simply because they act like all the other men or women in their group but also because they share the same appearance, because they *look* Awá or Q'eqchí'. All groups with relational identity display uniformed appearances as yet another way of neutralizing their differences, a strategy to constantly perform the very idea that they do not exist outside of the group. Historically, as male individuation increasingly became the identity counterpart of men's growing positions of power, it was women who predominantly kept the appearance that defined and differentiated the group from the rest, also allowing archaeologists to identify their areas of origin. Through the characteristics of some women's dress, exogamous relations have been traced back to the Mesolithic, but especially in the Bronze Age.[1] A much shorter leap back in history, to rural areas of the western European nineteenth century, for example, would also show how so-called *regional dress* continued to differentiate the women from a wide range of groups in a much higher proportion than the men. Or, if we turn to the "veil controversy", for example, we will find that the process of dress uniformization of contemporary Muslim populations is also more often associated with women than with men, at least when it comes to migrant communities established in foreign countries. In these cases, women, who characteristically have a more relational identity, are often put in charge of group identification (Cobo 2007, 2011). A superficial look at men's and women's appearances would seem to corroborate the claims of social discourse: in

---

[1] Among other studies, we can quote: Larsson (1988), Price et al. (2001: 601), Ruiz-Gálvez (1992: 220, 1996: 92), Wels-Weyrauch (1994), Jockenhövel (1990).

societies alien to modernity, only the women retain their *relational identity*. A more attentive approach, however, allows the proposal of a more complex account.

If we adopt an archaeologist's attitude and abandon social discourse to analyze, not what people say, but what they do, this automatically brings to light a different picture. An analysis of appearance in the Western world reveals that those who most uniformize their dress in modern society—thereby expressing their *relational identity*—are not women, but men with power. In fact, the more power men possess, the more they unify their appearance. Photographs of national parliaments in all countries, or of the European Parliament, the American Congress, the G-20 group, the United Nations, or of international banks, show all the men wearing a suit and tie, the *suit of power*. Acts of expression of social power of any type, whether academic, economic, or political, have made this suit mandatory and enshrined it as the norm.

As we have seen, due to the bidirectional interaction between subjects and objects, which I referred to at the beginning of this book, uniform appearance not only expresses but also *generates* ascription. It must be born in mind, especially, that identity operates through a complex combination of two *closed sets* of features: those of relational and those of individuated identity. Because the relationship between them is both structural and necessary, whenever a single feature of any one of these *sets* appears, it can be assumed that all the other defining features are also present. In this sense, uniform group appearance expresses *relational identity* and will therefore necessarily appear associated with all the other traits of this particular set, such as the use of metonymic signs, or the feeling of impotence, as well as the need to come under the protection of a higher instance, whose desires are to be satisfied in order to feel secure. If men with power standardize their dress, this means that they are activating the *relational block or set*. The only reason this is not acknowledged by them or other members of society at large is that men with power perform *relational identity* in an unconscious way, *denying* it both in their own lives and in the social discourse they themselves produce, and which we are all socialized in.

In fact, if we examine what the *individuated* men of modernity *do*, we will find that, unlike the women, they have developed a wide range of strategies to construct ascriptive or relational identities, which they use to establish emotional connection with their social group: football teams or sports teams in general, armies, nationalist identities, political parties, etc. Men are not linked to these groups rationally, but emotionally, their belonging is associated with uniform appearance, there exist a higher instance which the individual is subsumed into—because it is the sense of belonging that reinforces their identity (sports club, country, nation, political party, etc.)—and the signs that represent these instances are metonymic (trampling over a flag or the party acronym, or a scarf with the colors of the *other* team constitute as intolerable an affront as the profanation of a saint's image would be to its believers. As with any other relational identity, representation becomes an integral part of the represented). The less people recognize the importance of emotional connection as a mechanism of their own personal security—and therefore the less energy, time, and conscious effort they dedicate to understanding their own emotions—the more possibilities they have of establishing unequal gender relationships and of construing such unconscious relational identities, in order to generate the indispensable feeling of connection and belonging to the group.

Groups of collective ascription serve the purpose of compensating the insufficient emotional connection with the world that *dependent individuality* causes. For this reason, although some women have begun to join them recently, these groups have always been masculine. In fact, joining their ranks implies assimilating the logic and socio-emotional behavior that in our historical trajectory has characterized the needs of men (with *dependent individuality*) and not women. This has no connection whatsoever with the sexed bodies, but with the fact that, while women recognize their need for group connection explicitly and find multiple ways of performing it, men with dependent individuality do not.

And yet, there are also men who do not identify with such groups, which might lead us to the conclusion that their individuality is not based on a fantasy. This would certainly be the case, if, escaping the social norm and model of *dependent individuality* (what authors who explore masculinity have called *hegemonic masculinity*), these men granted the same importance and invested as much energy in the mechanisms of reason as they do in those of emotion.[2] Given how very infrequent this happens, however, as we shall see below, the most common situation is that these men in fact maintain their bonds and their sense of belonging through less obvious or visible means than ascribing to a football team. One of these peculiar forms of ascription—probably the least conscious and most unacknowledged of them all, insofar as it is the most contradictory with the discourse it proclaims—is identifying with the power group, as materialized by the uniformization of the particular suit-and-tie attire I have referred to above. What the *uniform of power* expresses (the need for group belonging) is in such contradiction with the discourse of those who wear it (a discourse of potency, superiority, personal autonomy, triumph, success, difference, etc.) that it requires a historical explanation. In order to propose one, we need to go back to the early stages of power, back in the remote times of prehistory.

As has been described, the so-called secondary product revolution was associated with the introduction of the horse, the ox, and certain technological innovations which signaled the definitive differentiation of the functions fulfilled by men and women, as well as their mobility. These innovations allowed the creation of commercial networks and the communitarian interaction of men who, significantly, displayed horse bit mouthpieces and carts (associated with mobility) as the most luxurious elements of their grave goods. At this moment certain European contexts also began to feature containers for alcoholic beverages, which according to Sherratt (1986: 6–7) were first associated with carts in the Baden Culture of the Danube area, during the first half of the third millennium BC (2700–2400 BC). These recipients attest to a new brand of hospitality linked to an increase in interregional contacts between men who were still very dependent on the mythical world but who already used weapons as instruments and symbols of power. Their dynamics have been defined as "prestige-goods economies", because these leaders would share both

---

[2] See note 8, Chap. 1.

ritual and esoteric knowledge (given the great importance of the mythical world and the sacred instance) and material goods to assert their privileged position (Rowlands 1980; Kristiansen 1982; Bradley 1984: 63; Renfrew and Cherry 1984; Ruiz-Gálvez 1992: 226).

At around 2500 BC, these early *chiefs'* individual burials began to spread across Western Europe. They tended to be inserted into earlier megalithic tombs (which had been collective burial sites) and were associated with highly standardized and luxurious grave goods: the earliest copper arrowheads appear next to these interred bodies, as do the earliest gold ornaments (proving their relationship with control over early metallurgy, the differentiation of wealth, and the emergence of a personalized type of power represented by weapons). These tombs also feature archer bracelets and buttons with a specific design (including a V-shaped perforation), both in ivory (which attests to trade with faraway regions and standardized dress) and a highly sophisticated and decorated type of luxury pottery known as *Bell Beaker pottery* (named after the inverted bell shape of one of its typical vases). Chemical analyses have proven that these vases were used to contain alcoholic beverages, particularly a blend of honey water, beer, and fruit wine (Sherratt 1987: 96). Interestingly, this very standardized set of male grave goods with very similar decorative patterns, and associated with the first elites, spread rapidly from Scotland to Sicily and from Portugal to Moravia (ibid.: 87). This means that at the exact same time as the earliest traces of male individuation—i.e. the first (small) emotional distance between some men and their social groups—emerged in Western Europe, those early chiefs began to unify their common appearance with each other. In other words, these men cut off their links with their own groups in the same measure—and, arguably, as a precondition for doing so—as they came to identify with another group, namely, men with power, in a separate socioeconomic sphere of interaction, and they displayed this new ascription through dress and material culture. Several authors consider this to represent the emergence of the "masculine ethos," which, enshrining the male warrior, lasted through prehistory and well into history (Treherne 1995: 108; Sherratt 1981: 299).

Still, such ascription is defined by identity contradictions shared by those who participate in it, as opposed to what happens when identity is only defined through bonds with one's own social group of origin. *Groups of chiefs* past and present are made up of men who feel stronger and more powerful than the rest of the group they belong to, what explains the impossibility of these chiefs of being aware (as well as because without writing, identity can never be reflexive) that their new ascription (to groups of chiefs) is actually determined by the impotence that defines their real position in the world and not by the increasing potency they feel toward it. In a similar process to that described for gender, as personal positions of power began to differentiate themselves within the group, the identities of those men who embodied them began to dissociate into two levels: first, a conscious level reflected by social discourse, associated with potency and characterized by increasing percentages of individual identity, and, second, an unconscious level (which remains invisible to discourse), which is characterized by an equally increased need to establish unequal gender relationships and by relational ascription to new groups. The purpose of this ascription is thus to compensate for the emotional distance inherent in exercising power in one's own group.

In European prehistory, ascription to male groups of *peers* became a trend as increasingly individuated men came to occupy positions of power (or vice versa). Objects associated with food and drink, dedicated to conviviality and the fraternity of warrior elites are, for example, typical of Iron Age grave goods (Ruiz-Gálvez 1992: 227). But, perhaps even more interestingly, in the same way as *Bell Beaker grave goods* included highly standardized ivory buttons indicating a common dress among the earliest elites, the grave goods of the chiefs at the head of *European Bronze Age society* tend to characteristically include so-called toilet articles. This was a set of bronze, horn, or bone combs, shaving tweezers, razors, mirrors, and awls (i.e., tattooing needles), which emerged around the same time in the second millennium in Central, Southern, Northern, and Northwestern Europe and which spread to the remaining European territories in the Late Bronze Age (Treherne 1995: 110). According to Kristiansen (1984), the set would have generated social identity through the alteration of physical appearance, defining warrior chiefs and their followers, that is (in the terms proposed in this book), creating new *relational identities,* expressed by a common appearance. It must be taken into consideration that, before the appearance of writing, interpersonal difference was not constructed through the mind but through the body and through actions (Treherne 1995), which redoubles the importance of bodily appearance as a fundamental identity strategy.

Marisa Ruiz-Gálvez (1998, 2009) has studied the socioeconomic trends which appeared in the Mediterranean and what we presently call Europe as a result of the collapse of the thirteenth-century B.C. Eastern Mediterranean palaces. Their fall forced a restructuring of commercial routes, hitherto controlled by these palaces, which were seized upon by persons in strategic areas to become middlemen between Europe and the Mediterranean. One of these key areas was modern-day Italy, whose position allowed it to establish and control, first, commercial routes between Central-Northern Europe and the East Mediterranean (through the amber route) and, second, between the opposite sides of the Mediterranean. Consequently this area saw the emergence of men enjoying a level of wealth and power which clearly distinguished them from the rest of the population, and which was, again, reflected by individuating features. It is worth noting that the grave goods associated with these early *businessmen* were made up of tableware, cooking ware (for hospitality and conviviality), and such elements as shaving razors. These were associated with esthetic codes related to beard grooming (Ruiz-Gálvez 1998: 107). Power became associated with uniform appearance, also requiring displays of the chief's condition as an adult male (remember that the beard is also the attribute to represent God the Father in the European myth of legitimation par excellence).

Another interesting Bronze Age feature is the iconography on Late Bronze Age stelae in the Southeast Iberian Peninsula (Galán 1993), an area which, at that very moment, saw numerous Eastern Mediterranean merchant incursions up those rivers which allowed inland commercial penetration. Along the courses of these navigable rivers, stelae decorated with carvings featured mostly masculine motifs associated with war and power, such as arches, arrows, swords, shields, helmets, carts, and, in a great number of cases, (bronze) mirrors, attesting to the importance of appearance as a fundamental parameter in construing the identities of those early warriors and *businessmen*. Far from anecdotal, this fact is fundamental to understanding the ways in which that initial *fantasy of individuality* was constructed. By identifying with each other as members of the *group of the powerful*, and by visualizing that ascription through their appearance, these men counterbalanced the *deficit* in the identification with their own ethnic groups which is inherent to individuality. Only by ascribing to a new group could they abandon identification with their previous one. Women retained relational identity within their own groups, as was visually expressed by their *regional dress*, whereas men performed the same identity by linking up with men from other groups. This shift operated unconsciously and remained invisible to members of their own groups, so men appeared to have *substituted* it for individuality. The more conscious and visible their individuation was inside their own groups, the more unconscious and denied became the relational identity they performed through links with other men in their same situation. The suit and tie would be the most recent expression of this mechanism. Between prehistory and modernity, a number of unconsciously ascribed identities have allowed men to construe their fantasy of increasing individuality, providing them the possibility of considering themselves more and more autonomous and independent from the group.

Let us consider now those men who enjoy the greatest economic and political power in contemporary Western society: bankers, financiers, owners of multinationals, and premier political figures. They happen to rule the world at this precise moment, so their subjective perception of their own power would appear to be anything but a fantasy. And yet, significantly, in view of the process described above, they constitute the single most unified-looking group, with their suits and ties signaling their need to ascribe to groups of belonging. But if this group (unknowingly) performs a relational identity, we might ask ourselves, what would the idealized protective instance be? In some cases we could say money, in others power. In either case these men's self-esteem, self-confidence, and sense of privilege and of difference from others all rely on obtaining and retaining them (money and/or power). Although this dependency forces them to adopt an *object* position and to become mere vehicles of the desires of the so-called logic of the market or of many different intersecting interests, their feeling of personal distinction makes them feel so privileged by comparison to the rest that they become unaware of their own subjection. These men are as unaware as hunter-gatherers are as they go about interpreting their world through the logic of the sacred and submitting to its desires, feeling they are the *chosen* ones. The desires that these men with power pursue may have no connection whatsoever with their emotional needs, which they might even be unaware of. In fact, the extent of that ignorance will dictate the measure of their need to belong to these groups, for only that very belonging—and the unequal gender relationships they establish—allows them to generate an emotional connection strong enough to sustain the *fantasy* on which their *individuality* rests.

Some contexts favor more subtle strategies, such as the scientific and academic community I belong to myself. In academia, the suit and tie are mandatory at any event where the powers directing the community represent themselves, from a doctoral thesis to any conference of a certain level of importance. And yet, it could rightly be argued that, unlike bankers and politicians, academics do not dress in that way on a day-to-day basis (and that young generations do so less and less), suggesting that its representatives' identities might obey different dynamics. Admittedly, there are some differences between the academic world and the power groups referred to above, for academics specialize precisely in the use of the instrument of individuality par excellence: reason. But the academic world is nonetheless utterly fraught with identity traps. The main one could be defined as the *idealization* of reason itself, as the great majority of academics are governed by a relationship with knowledge closer to the level of *belief* than to that of true reason (Midgley 2004). In a world which claims to be defined by constant questioning and where reason would seem to impose a permanent state of doubt, paradoxically, established paradigms (the ways of thinking which direct power in each discipline) are not easily questioned. Against the claims of its discourse, critical thinking is not so welcome in the academic world. As Kuhn (1962) once proved, it is so difficult to question and debunk the scientific *truths* of a certain time that to substitute them for others constitutes a true revolution, after which new *truths* duly appear as articles of faith to *believe* in. The problem lies not only in the content which each scientific discipline considers to be the unquestionable *truth* at any given time but also in the very value of *truth* which science is identified with, as has also been pointed out above. At this moment, the main mechanism sustaining and reinforcing the *fantasy of individuality* is the application of the principles of positive or natural science to the study of human societies. There is a positive correlation between *dependent individuality* and *positivism*, for those who deny the importance of emotions in their own security mechanisms cannot imagine how this dimension could possibly operate in the phenomena they study. This is the very reason why they identify the human with nonhuman instances or even with machines. We shall return to this point below.

To go back to the question of appearance in the scientific world, it is true that professionals of reason do not usually unify their appearance in their everyday lives. This reflects their shared assumption, caused by their constant immersion in the world of thought, that deep down inside, they are all different from each other: in their view, that difference would lie not in what they do but in the ideas they are capable of generating, in their mind and the core that constitutes their *self* (*cogito ergo sum*). Although true intellectuals do exist—people defined by their critical capacities and autonomous thought—who do not fit into the model I am about to describe (and who, incidentally, are not always part of the academic world), more than 20 years in this profession have taught me that the *fantasy of individuality* has some of its greatest representatives in the academic world. Although their actions might suggest the opposite, most academics firmly believe that their individuality rests solely on the particularity of their thoughts and the creative potential of their ideas. As the larger society that they are a part of also shares this belief (and sees the world through the discourse that they produce), academics are constantly reassured by social recognition and valorization. But, once again, if we focus on the material culture governing the academic world's logic of physical appearance, we will find that paradoxically, though unsurprisingly at this point in the argument, the more any society idealizes scientific knowledge, the more it resorts to *religious* and *ceremonial* symbols to dress those who represent it. No other present-day profession uses the kind of religious and ritualized dress that defines so-called academic dress. Made up, at its simplest, of a mortarboard and robe, it is used at all *rites of passage* related to studies in the United States, where the *truth* of positive science is *idealized,* along with that of sociobiological currents applied to the study of human phenomena. In Spain, although the number of ceremonies where professors are expected to wear them is increasing—following the trend toward Anglo-Saxon models—until recently these outfits were only used at the highest level of academic prestige, such as the granting of an *honoris causa* doctorate. Participating in one of these ceremonies reinforces a fully codified ancient ritual, where robes, mozzettas (capes), long embroidered cuffs, and head gear necessarily remind us of the clerical dress they come from. The academic world is the institution *par excellence* of the mythical belief in the God of reason, precisely when it does not operate as reason, but as the mere reproduction of learned formulae and strategies of power, thus preventing the necessary emotional distance for critique to come into play. The phrase *temples of knowledge*, which society has reserved for the most prestigious universities in the world, reveals the trap I am referring to. The fact that rational knowledge can be considered the object of adoration is telling about the levels of personal identification (always an uncritical stance) that inform the academic world's relationship with reason. Through the sense of belonging to its power circles, an unconscious type of relational relationship is performed. This sense of belonging reassures its members and makes them feel strong and privileged over all other people, and it instills a sense of being true bearers of the secret of survival, a certainty about the true dynamics of the world, as revealed by reason. However, as in any other case where groups feel that they are in possession of a truth that proves their superiority, which reassures them that they are the chosen ones, the full *set* of relational traits is activated. And if this happens, the group's survival strategy will consist in discovering and satisfying the desires of an instance which is alien to themselves, blatantly contradicting the alleged autonomy of the individuality they take such pride in.

Thus, the academic world reaches the highest peak of the contradiction between the conscious and the unconscious, the recognized and the muffled, and the search for power and the deepening of knowledge. Because the academic world ultimately specializes in construing the discourse that sustains our social order, positions of power within it are generally (although there are always exceptions) occupied by those who firmly *believe* in this discourse as *true* and on a daily basis *act* the dissociation and denial that lie at the core of the *fantasy of individuality*. It is therefore no coincidence that, if we analyze the proportion of men and women in these positions (as in any power structure, whatever the type), the number of women decreases as we approach the top (Arranz Lozano 2004; García de León 2002, 2005; García de León and García de Cortázar 1998, 2001). Tribunals, editorial committees, contracting commissions, etc., all operate a filtering, as effective as it is unconscious, of those who will sustain and reinforce the discourse most efficaciously. And, generally, women cannot, and do not usually desire to, afford to sustain the fantasy which this discourse is built upon. The next chapter is devoted to this fundamental point.

References

Arranz Lozano, F. (2004). Las mujeres y la Universidad española: estructuras de dominacion y disposiciones feminizadas en el profesorado universitario. *Política y Sociedad, 41*(2), 223–242.
Bradley, R. (1984). *The social foundations of prehistoric Europe*. Londres: Longman.
Cobo, R. (2007). Multiculturalismo y nuevas formas de violencia patriarcal. In C. Amorós & L. P. Kubissa (Eds.), *Feminismo y multiculturalismo* (pp. 71–84). Madrid: Instituto de la Mujer.
Cobo, R. (2011). *Hacia una nueva política sexual. Las mujeres ante la reacción patriarcal*. Catarata: Madrid.
Galán, E. (1993). *Estelas, paisaje y territorio en el Bronce Final del Suroeste*. Revista Complutum, Extra N° 3.
García de León, M. A. (2005). *La excelencia científica. (Hombres y mujeres en las Reales Academias)*. Madrid: Instituto de la Mujer.
García de León, M. A., & García de Cortázar, M. L. (1998). *Mujeres en minoría. Sobre las catedráticas de Universidad*. Madrid: Editorial CIS.
García de León, M. A. & María Luisa García de Cortázar (Coords.) (2001). *Las académicas (Profesorado universitario y género)*. Madrid: Instituto de la Mujer.
García de León, M. A. (2002). *Herederas y heridas (Elites profesionales femeninas)*. Valencia: Cátedra.
Jockenhövel, A. (1990). Räumliche Mobilität von Personen in der mittleren Bronzezeit des westlichen Mitteleuropa. *Germania, 69*, 49–62.
Kristiansen, K. (1982). The formation of tribal systems in later european prehistory: Northern Europe 4000-500 B.C. In C. Renfrew, M. J. Rowlands, & B. A. Seagraves (Eds.), *Theory and explanation in Archaeology* (pp. 241–280). Cambridge: Cambridge University Press.
Kristiansen, K. (1984). Ideology and material culture: and archaeological perspective. In M. Spriggs (Ed.), *Marxist perspectives in Archaeology* (pp. 72–100). Cambridge: Cambridge University Press.
Kuhn, T. S. (1962). *The structure of scientific revolutions*. Chicago: University of Chicago Press.
Larsson, L. (1988). Aspects of exchange in Mesolithic Societies. In B. Hardh, L. Larsson, D. Olausson, & R. Petré (Eds.), *Trade and exchange in Prehistory. Studies in honour of Berta Stjernquist, Series In 8°, N° 16* (pp. 25–32). Lund: Acta Archaeologica Lundensia.
Midgley, M. (2004). *The myths we live by*. Londres/New York: Routledge Classics.
Price, T. D., Bentley, R. A., Lüning, J., Gronenborn, D., & Wahl, J. (2001). Prehistoric human migration in the *Linearbandkeramik* of Central Europe. *Antiquity, 75*, 593–603.
Renfrew, C., & Cherry, J. F. (Eds.). (1984). *Peer polity interaction and socio-political change*. Cambridge: Cambridge University Press.
Rowlands, M. J. (1980). Kinship, alliance and exchange in the european Bronze Age. In J. Barret & R. Bradley (Eds.), *Settlement and society in the British Later Bronze Age, British Archaeological Reports (British Series) 83* (pp. 15–55). Oxford: Archaeopress.
Ruiz-Gálvez, M. L. (1992). La novia vendida: orfebrería, herencia y agricultura. *SPAL, 1*, 219–251.
Ruiz-Gálvez, M. L. (1996). La orfebrería y su significado. In *El oro y la orfebrería prehistórica de Galicia* (pp. 87–98). Lugo: Diputación Provincial y Museo Provincial.
Ruiz-Gálvez, M. L. (1998). Peripheral, but not that much…¡. In V. Oliveira Jorge (Ed.), *Intercâmbio e Comércio: As "Economías" da Idade de Bronze (I)*. Monography of Trabalhos de Arqueología 10 (pp. 101–113).
Ruiz-Gálvez, M. L. (2009). ¿Qué hace un micénico como tú en un sitio como éste? Andalucía entre el colapso de los palacios y la presencia semita. *Trabajos de Prehistoria, 66*(2), 93–118.
Sherratt, A. (1981). Plough and pastoralism: Aspects of the secondary products revolution. In I. Hodder, G. Isaac, & N. Hammond (Eds.), *Pattern of the past. Studies in honour of David Clarke* (pp. 261–303). Cambridge: Cambridge University Press.
Sherratt, A. (1986). Wool, wheels and plughmarks: Local developments or outside introductions in Neolithic Europe? *Institute of Archaeology Bulletin, 23*, 1–15.

Sherratt, A. (1987). Cups that cheered. In W. H. Waldren & R. C. Kennard (Eds.), *Bell beakers of the Western Mediterranean. Definition, interpretation, theory and new site data.* British Archaeological Reports (International Series) 331(i): 81–113.The Oxford International Conference, 1986. Oxford, Archaeopress.

Treherne, P. (1995). The warrior's beauty: the masculine body and self-identity in Bronze-Age Europe. *Journal of European Archaeology, 3*(1), 105–144.

Wels-Weyrauch, U. (1994). In Grab enhalten, im Leben Getragen – Tracht und Schmuck der Frau. In A. Jockenhövel & W. Kubach (Eds.), *Bronzezeit in Dutschland* (pp. 59–64). Stuttgart: Theiss.

Chapter 9
Dependent Individuality and *Independent* Individuality

9.1 Dependent Individuality

The ideas developed so far in this book could be summarized as follows: while at the start of all historical trajectories men and women's identities were equally relational, over time men gradually acquired increasingly individual traits. These traits developed to an extent that was correlative to the number of phenomena that men could explain rationally and control technologically. As the number of these phenomena increased, so did those men's perception of the differences between themselves and their own groups, which they came to identify with less and less. But it is not possible for human beings to break off from their own group completely, for, if they were ever to gain true autonomy, they would perceive their own impotence before the powerful universe they inhabit. So, as men in positions of power began to define themselves through individual traits—i.e., traits of potency and capacity of agency—they began to satisfy their need for bonds by displaying a number of unacknowledged and *denied* strategies which remained concealed by social discourse: one of these strategies was to establish gender relationships where women (who retained the *relational identity* which had once characterized the whole group) were put in charge of forging bonds. A second strategy was to substitute the bonds that had once linked them to their original group for alliances with a wide range of new peers inside or outside their own groups. The contradiction inherent in the fact that both forms of identity could possibly coexist within the same person is systematically *denied* by men with *dependent individuality,* who recognize only the individual part of themselves—and by a social discourse which claims that autonomous reason and individuals can exist—. Yet, despite that denial, the contradiction persists (see Fig. 9.1).

Therefore, since human beings cannot possibly break off from their own group while at the same time retaining a feeling of safety and the certainty that they will survive, we may conclude that *relational identity is always active in all people to its greatest degree.* As well as this, *varying percentages of individuation* may exist alongside it, for, unlike relational identity, individual identity is dispensable and can

RELATIONAL IDENTITY	DEPENDENT INDIVIDUALITY
MEN AND WOMEN in egalitarian *societies*. WOMEN (in all other societies until modernity) Logic of MYTH Importance is given to:	(Patriarchal) MEN Logic of HISTORY Importance is given to:
Value of stability and permanencies	Value of change
Value of emotion	Advance of reason
Importance of human bonds	Importance of technology
DENIED (yet indispensable) ⟵	REASSURES THE GROUP (recognized)

Fig. 9.1 Diagram of *dependent individuality*

present itself in different measures, depending on the position of specialization or power that each person occupies. *Dependent individuality* can be described as an iceberg of which only a small part is visible, luminous and brilliant, and seemingly floating and existing by itself before an adverse ocean. But, like an iceberg, the appearance of floating graciously over the waters can only be construed because it relies on an immense sustentation, much larger than the visible part which, since it remains hidden, submerged beneath the surface, cannot glisten in the sunrays or compete in size or beauty before those who admiringly watch the iceberg from the water surface.

Dependent individuality operates on the belief that its own security can rely exclusively on mechanisms of reason and change (such as science or technology), since these are the only ones it consciously operates on. For this reason, at the same time as they began to control the world through these mechanisms, men stopped granting importance and devoting time and effort to emotional mechanisms (such as bonding, connecting with others, etc.). But since they are indispensable, these mechanisms continued operating in men, albeit at an unconscious level, and as a result their own emotional world became for them a black hole—a bundle that caught up their needs, their weaknesses, their insecurities, and their fears—all of which they increasingly failed to recognize. The black hole of men's emotions became more obscure the more power they felt through the mechanisms of reason. For this very reason, anything they had (or have) the possibility to perceive on an emotional level could never (or can never) be identified as a source of security and potency but, rather, as the exact opposite. The emotional world of men is inhabited by that which they most fear and therefore most deny, the proof of their own insecurity before the world. For this reason, men with this type of identity can only

9.1 Dependent Individuality

sustain emotional relationships that conceal this contradiction and as long as they do not shed light on what their denial hides. This makes these men with *dependent individuality* (so-called hegemonic masculinity) incapable of sustaining emotional relationships unless they are pervaded by inequality and never fail to cast back images of their own power and security: they establish such relationships with their wives and children but also with their employees, students, collaborators, or admirers, who are expected to assist them in acting out the fantasy that they do value their emotional world. The problem is that this power *bias* that taints their emotional relationships constitutes in itself a trap. Since these men are never confronted with their own fears, insecurities, dreads, and impotencies, they are systematically prevented from either keeping these at bay or solving them and from recognizing their real needs and desires. Finally—and paradoxically—sustaining this type of power (economic, political, academic, or personal) subjects men to dynamics that are, for the most part, not of their own choice and which might not even satisfy them in the slightest. But the reinforcement of these dynamics has come to play such a central part in construing the fantasy of their personal power that they have become vital. Caught in this trap, men are forced to mobilize vast amounts of desire and energy to keep up appearances, leaving little or no space for the true needs of being, for, among other reasons, these are no longer even visible to the individuals themselves.

Dependent individuality operates on a type of narcissism which places the person who embodies it at the center of everyone's attention, as it demands constant recognition as a prerequisite for security, in this way manifesting the fundamental insecurity that defines this type of person's emotional world: nonhuman nature is explained through rational dynamics, which are seen as autonomous and independent from whoever thinks them. But when it comes to emotional dynamics, these are always made to revolve around oneself, so as to compensate for the insecurities they generate: here, the sun must continue to orbit around the Earth. Emotional dynamics are as unknown to *dependent individuality* as those governing thunder, and hailstorms are to hunter-gatherers, and in order to explain them, dependent individuals project their own behavior onto them and believe the entire universe to revolve around themselves. Narcissism, egotism, self-centeredness, or whatever we wish to call it always attests to the emotional insecurities of those who display these traits. Only if one is secure enough in one's knowledge and in control of one's own dynamics can autonomy be granted to those of others, and this applies as much to reason as it does to emotion.

Social sciences, that is, the discourse generated by those who have this type of identity and who therefore wield power in the academic world, have only seen the external, brilliant, and attractive part of the iceberg, identifying *dependent individuality* with mere *individuality* and associating it with the identity developed by men throughout history. The social sciences cannot unveil the cheating construction underlying it, for those who construct discourse cannot possibly see this (*denied*) part in themselves. For this reason, researchers with *dependent individuality* identify *true* and scientific knowledge with positive science, equating the way in which human and nonhuman nature operate, which, in other words, means that they ignore the emotional component. The same mechanism used by hunter-gatherers to generate a feeling of security is repeated, although turned on its head: the dynamics of the sphere which provides security are projected to explain those where insecurity is felt, in order to construe the fantasy that both are under control. Hunter-gatherers explain nonhuman nature by projecting social dynamics onto it. Patriarchal science explains social dynamics by projecting onto it the dynamics of nonhuman nature. To contain the advance of insecurity, phenomena that cannot be controled are explained through the dynamics of what can be controled, unwittingly attesting to the perfect efficacy of identity mechanisms.

However, if *dependent individuality* is the type of identity that sustains power in present-day society, and if women are increasingly gaining access to positions of power, could we say that women are developing this type of identity and therefore achieving equality? To answer this question, we must turn back to the historical process and analyze the complex situation faced by women at the arrival of modernity.

9.2 Independent Individuality

As we have seen, until the arrival of modernity, the Western world's entire historical process was characterized by a growing division of functions and the work specialization of men, in a set of dynamics which, once established, boosted their own logic at an increasing pace. As socioeconomic complexity grew, the key of security was increasingly placed on the changes carried out by men, setting off the dynamics of an increased acceleration: the greater the socioeconomic complexity, the greater the individuation, and therefore, the more changes, which in turn, created greater complexity (I will not judge the conflicts or contradictions inherent in these changes from the economic or social point of view).

However, with the arrival of modernity, the accelerated process of division of functions and work specialization reached a critical point, for most men already occupied specialized positions, and, for the first time in history, the possibility that women might also carry out specialized work could contribute to the trend toward increased complexity. In turn, growing numbers of women from bourgeois families, trained in reading and writing, developed such strong individual traits that they could no longer find an adequate space for expression in convents. Through reason, they reclaimed an application of the egalitarian principles claimed by a society that was allegedly guided by reason itself.[1] But this claim began to reveal the *fantasy* sustaining a social order which stated that *reason* was the only instrument of liberation and emancipation. Men could not possibly allow women to engage in the world through reason, not because they failed to recognize the rights women were legitimately entitled to but, basically and essentially, because if women stopped fulfilling the function of emotional sustentation which they had so far carried out, men would

---

[1] Valcárcel (2008: 63) defines feminism as the "unwanted child" of Enlightenment.

be forced to recognize that they could not rely solely on reason for their sense of security. Without the mechanisms of emotion, without a sense of belonging, and without bonds, men would feel lost. They would have to begin to recognize everything they had so far *denied*, a denial which had only been possible because women had fulfilled that function for them. Men refused to recognize this because the entire social order had been built on a logic based on that very denial, which both men and women continued to be socialized into. This contradiction explains the relatively high number of intelligent men with power who endorse rational and explicit discourses in favor of equality with women while sustaining unequal relationships with their own partners, truly unaware of the contradiction between their discourse and practices. As a result of all this, and from the very start of modernity, women were increasingly subjected to an intrinsically contradictory demand, which required, on the one hand, that they individuate—to keep up with the social order's technologizing and specializing trends—and, on the other hand, that they did not individuate—to allow men to retain their own specialized positions of power. These contradictory demands continue to be pressed to this day, making it highly complicated for many women to keep the mental equilibrium in their lives, as discourse states one thing, while the majority of men who rationally defend that same discourse continue to emotionally demand the opposite.

As we have seen, unlike men, women in the Western world had not developed their individuality gradually. Only members of the elite had developed some traits and had been socially aborted through their internment in convents. Most women conformed to the normative model of socialization, passing onto their daughters an identity (and therefore, desires) which encouraged them to specialize in strengthening bonds within the group. Men, on the other hand, had gradually been released of training in this ability so that they could specialize in developing formal and rational logic. This differentiation had been transmitted through the socialization of men and women in increasingly divergent forms of identity, reinforcing and strengthening either one type of identity or the other. When, on arriving at modernity, women modified the path that had characterized them throughout history and began to individuate (developing specialized functions associated with rational thought and the technological control which had, so far, only been developed by men), they came up against a very different social scenario from the one that had saluted men's gradual process of individuation: unlike men, women could not rely on someone else to guarantee their bonds with the group for them, so their individuality could not possibly be founded on the fantasy that reason was the only key to security. The only way women would be able to develop their own individuality within society was by relying on themselves, without any specialized assistance and without any tricks.

This means that, once they specialized in reason and technology, individuated women were forced to recognize what their masculine counterparts *denied*: that if bonds with the group and emotional connection are abandoned, it is impossible to become individuated. Only by feeling can life begin to be thought of, for bonds, and not reason, are what render life meaningful. It is *sensing* that *makes sense*. Without feelings, we are overcome by loneliness and a sense of unrewarded effort, and no personal drive can possibly carry the heavy burden that living turns into. Individuality is a type of identity which subjects people to constant demands, because, as we have seen, it is based on change and the need to endlessly define the desires we identify with the individual *self*. Individuality comprises anxiety, searching, instability, and unstoppable and inevitable transformation. That is a load too heavy to be carried on one's own. It cannot be done. It is too cold inside individuality, for it leaves human beings naked before the universe. This burden has to be compensated for with the stability of permanencies, with the references constituted by links, and with the warmth and protection of emotions. It is not possible to fool ourselves, to construe any fantasy for ourselves if we are truly faced with the world, without someone to give us shelter from it and hide from us its true dimension. Modernity thus confronted women with a very different situation from that facing men. Women had to become aware of the fact that they could only fulfil a specialized function by making an effort to maintain bonds, that they could only develop reason by granting due importance to emotion, and that they could only develop an individuated identity by maintaining their relational identity. The iceberg had no other choice but to recognize the enormous weight that has to be carried to be able to shine on the surface. This is what I call *independent individuality* (Fig. 9.2). It does not rely on external support to construct itself. It does not fool itself, it is not based on relations of power or inequality, and it does not deny its own needs but pays a very high price to construe itself, for it demands being *aware of the contradiction* inherent in the feeling of security in modernity, the very contradiction that *dependent individuality* denies and hides.

Independent individuality consists in consciously conjugating a maximal percentage of individuality with a maximal of relational identity, granting equal importance to both. It stems from the perception of security, strength, and potency generated by a rational understanding of the world's dynamics, as well as that generated by human bonds, devoting energy, time, and dedication to both. It is built on

INDEPENDENT INDIVIDUALITY	
QUITE SOME WOMEN (since modernity) SOME MEN	
Value of stability and permanencies	Value of changes
Value of emotion	Advance of "reason"
Importance of human links	Importance of technology
Its importance cannot be *denied* RECOGNIZED	**REASSURES THE GROUP (RECOGNIZED)**

Fig. 9.2 Diagram of *independent individuality*

the acceptance that only by recognizing their essential impotence can human beings acquire any power. How to balance so apparent an inconsistency? It can be done only by understanding and accepting the contradictions it rests on.

Independent individuality catches people up in a constant, inevitable, and everyday contradiction, for they consciously and actively live and perform both the set of traits of their relational identity and those of their individuated identity. And so, on the one hand, independent individuals devote themselves to recurrent tasks centered around known spaces, such as domestic ones, where time is cyclical, change is unwanted, and space constitutes the main parameter in imposing order onto reality. And on the other hand, these individuals carry out professional activities that require constant changes and where time constitutes the fundamental ordering parameter. Persons with this *independent individuality* perceive themselves, on the one hand, as *self*-constructed through the changes they have sought and made in life, but, on the other hand, they feel lost unless they perceive themselves as part of a network of relations. This is the reason maternity continues to be a nonrenounceable strategy of identity reassurance for many women, no matter how individuated they are; and it is the reason their intellectual autonomy must be supplemented with highly intimate relationships (with their partners or friends).

This same contradiction explains why a woman can feel she is the *subject* in the relationships she establishes, secure about her capacity for action and decision, of her agency and potency, while at the same time she can place herself systematically in the *object* position, dressing up and putting on makeup to be desired, or removing some parts of her hair and having other parts of it dyed to appear young. She not only needs to be considered intelligent but also pretty. The same contradictions make many women incapable of preventing their emotional problems from uncontrollably interrupting their concentration at work, whereas to many men, work is precisely a way of escaping emotional problems. Even stronger is the constant conflict unsettling those women who are trapped between prioritizing their own desires and the desires of those who constitute the terms of their relational identity (parents, husbands, children). Solving this can cause guilt and ambivalences never experienced by *dependent individuality*, which decidedly prioritizes one's own desire and always places those (men) who perform it, without a doubt or shame, in the *subject* position. In Fig. 9.3, I highlight several of the most common terms of this contradiction.

As they grapple with these contradictions, women tend to experience them as personal inabilities, when in fact these are inherent in the type of individuality that characterizes us in modernity. These contradictions cannot be escaped. In fact, they are the condition for the most powerful form of identity that exists, for it forces human beings to recognize what they really *are*, allowing them to accept that only by recognizing weakness can one attain real strength, that only by recognizing impotence can one achieve real power, that only by acknowledging our dependence on others can we become independent, that only by knowing our own fears can our desires be revealed, that only by feeling part of a network of interactions can we define our own particularity, and that only by recognizing the desires of others in the same terms as our own can we construct autonomy and equality. *Independent*

INDEPENDENT INDIVIDUALITY	
RELATIONAL IDENTITY: its core is placed at the relationships established	**INDIVIDUALIZED IDENTITY**: its core is established at the "self"
Change is valued negatively: recurrent activities	Change is valued positively: specialized activities
Space constitutes the most visible axis for ordering reality	**Time** constitutes the most visible axis in ordering reality.
NO POWER IS FELT BEFORE THE WORLD	**POWER IS FELT BEFORE THE WORLD**
Trust in destiny and survival is placed in a man with whom a dependent and subordinate relationship is established	Trust in destiny and survival isplaced in initiative and personal work
Security based on the confidence of having been chosen by a man:OBJECT POSITION	Security based on being the agent of controlled action:SUBJECT POSITION
No desires are generated for oneself, and instead, there is permanent concern about finding out and satisfying those of the *man* who provides security	Personal identity manifests itself through awareness of particular desires and the ability to satisfy them

Fig. 9.3 *Independent individuality* combines in the same person the contradictory traits of relational identity and individuality

individuality constitutes the most potent type of identity that has ever existed, because it allows (and forces) us to develop our full capacities and potentialities as humans, those relating to reason and to emotion alike. This way, fully equipped with all instruments, we are granted enough force to recognize the truth: that the universe overcomes us; that only by bonding with the community we belong to can we feel strong; that it is not possible to feel strength, security, or power if we are alone; and that *individuality is just a fantasy.*

But the price for embodying this identity mode is high, for it requires accepting contradiction as our inevitable condition. The psychic suffering that provokes is usually further increased by the difficulties encountered by many women in establishing relationships, in despite of being so conscious of their need for bonds: since, with varying degrees, most men continue to develop forms of *dependent individuality*, the more individuated a woman is, the harder it will be for her to find a partner. Men will continue to prefer women who still clearly prioritize the *relational set* (although they might have specialized jobs and higher education, and, therefore, a certain degree of individuality). This is, in my opinion, the present situation for many couples who perceive themselves as *egalitarian* because they both happen to have specialized jobs, but who actually are not. Within these relationships, the women duplicate their tasks and take on not only their own work responsibilities but also the emotional support and the sustainment of bonds for both partners, while the men continue to focus their energies exclusively on specialized social functions, related to reason and power. An egalitarian relationship requires that both parties handle the contradiction and the richness of *independent individuality* equally, which is still difficult to achieve and happens only very rarely.

9.2 Independent Individuality

In order to build a truly *independent individuality*, it is crucial to understand the traps of social discourse, the nature of the denial it rests on, and to renounce the type of *truth* it preaches. This is far more complicated than it might appear, for we all *are* social order—because our subjectivity is construed through its imperatives—so the way in which we understand the world is, to varying degrees, modeled by that very regime of truth. In fact, I would say that the way in which the contradictions of *independent individuality* manifest themselves at present are, in most cases, shaped by the *relational* demands of patriarchal discourse. The contradictions currently experienced by most women are still caused by the very position that this order places them in (demanding that they run in two opposite directions at the same time), and not by those other contradictions described as inherent to *independent individuality*. For example, the growing sexualization and objectification in the Anglo-Saxon world observed by Walter (2010) (which could be extrapolated to the entire Western world) have been established with the enthusiastic participation of many women who consider it a product of their own sexual liberation (without noticing that men never put themselves in that position). Another case in point is the fact that many highly individuated women continue to see settling down with a partner—something which is all the more unlikely the more individuated they are—as the *only* possible way of satisfying the emotional links demanded by their *relational* part. Indeed, many individuated heterosexual women experience the lack of a partner as an *unacceptable social fault (therefore as a subjective one)*, which often fills them with anxiety and the feeling of *being incomplete*. Through all sorts of mechanisms, social discourse will transmit to them—and they will actually come to believe it—that they do not know how to love or establish relationships unless they have a fixed partner, and they will continue to put pressure on themselves to establish one, albeit on unsatisfactory terms. Even if they do have one, and they also have a family, they might feel that they are not good enough mothers or wives, because they take out time and attention for their professional activities. But neither will they achieve approval in these, for unless they set out from a dissociated logic, they will be considered *too emotional*, insufficiently dedicated to work, or incapable of mastering the scientific accuracy needed to understand the *true*, and exclusively rational, dynamics governing the world.

And yet, the couple—the *norm* for relationships in an order based on dissociation requiring two complementary terms to be construed—is merely one of the possibilities for establishing emotional links and belonging to the group when that order is put into question. In fact, profound friendships can provide a degree of bonding, company, and emotional support much greater than those afforded by many couples,[2] but a large part of women cannot contemplate this possibility as desirable because they continue to see themselves through the spectrum of social discourse.

---

[2] Giddens (1991: 90) defined friendship as the only *pure* relationship, not motivated by any interests or submitted to any obligation, and whose only reward is the relationship in itself. In the text I don't make any references to sexual relationships as it seems clear that a stable partner is not necessary to be able to sustain these.

In fact, building strong emotional and intellectual bonds is fundamental in this identity mode, for it is hard to understand the disappointment that a society guided by the logic of *dependent individuality* can generate in those who live their lives through *independent individuality*. These people (mostly women, as we have seen, but also some men) are constantly forced to interact in dynamics that are governed by appearances, in turn sustained by denied contradictions. For them, social interaction becomes a sort of theater play, where every day they enter a scene which, offstage and on their way home, they recognize as a fantasy, alien to real life. For this reason, they are overcome by perplexity when they understand that the social discourse which we are all socialized in states that the *truth is that script* and not what happens when they arrive home; or when it states that men with *dependent individuality* and women with *independent individuality* have the same chances of achieving political, economic, or academic power, even when those men who achieve it have so obviously often done by placing the responsibility of their emotional world on the women who accompany them (the men thereby being able to devote most of their energies, their time, and their concentration to their specialized work). They will also have to hear that women are more emotional and weaker than men, simply because the latter only show their fragility and weakness when they return home or that women are more dependent than men, when men's enormous difficulty to live on their own is as ubiquitous as the frequency with which women with *independent individuality* are forced to deal with solitude. And so on and so forth. Our own day-to-day experience tells us all that none of these statements is true, and yet we continue to reinforce them as if they were, revealing that the *truth* that a society believes in can be the opposite of lived experience without this causing it to be questioned, for we are taught to understand the world in a certain way, which is associated with the power ruling the social order we are a part of.

For this reason, those who do not wish to reinforce the *denial* underlying discourse, and decide to question it, need to establish strong alliances among themselves, interwoven into serious intellectual and emotional commitments. Otherwise, they could be overcome by disconcertment, confusion, and suffering, as is the case with so many women (and with, as yet, unfortunately very few men) who continue to assess the *maladjustment* between their own ways of being and the logic of power as a personal problem of theirs or a symptom of their own shortcomings. Those who have not been able to build that network of support, nor understand the traps underpinning *dependent individuality*, may even feel a certain envy toward men with that identity mode who occupy positions of power. Everything appears much easier for (that type of) men: they do not feel either conflict or shame in pursuing their own desires, so these appear much easier to satisfy. Also, since these men dedicate nearly all their energy to work and reason, they have much greater chances of achieving high positions of success and power. As if that were not enough, they always find a woman who is prepared to look after, understand, and sustain their unfathomable emotional world and (although this is beginning to be shared) to take care (or at least, take greater care) of tasks related to children and the household. It is inevitable to have envied this at some point. But envy vanishes once we understand that these men's contradictions basically differ from those of individuated women not in that they do not exist but in that they are not acknowledged by them, which dramatically decreases their chances of being solved. And if we take a closer look at these men's identity mode—in the light that the thick veil of patriarchal discourse constantly tries to block—we will find them constantly submitted to desires that are not of their own choice due to their need to identify with the (power) dynamics that provide them security. We will be able to verify how generally incapable these men are of satisfying their most intimate needs, due to their utter unawareness of them. We will find that, in most cases, they can only break off from a dysfunctional relationship when they find another one to substitute it, because they are not *emotionally autonomous*, or that their need to sustain unequal relationships prevents them from allowing themselves to be transformed by rich and profound interaction with peers. Envy of those men vanishes as soon as we observe *what they perform* and not what *patriarchal discourse says* about the individuality developed by men with power.

I have insisted that there are also highly individuated men who do not present this *dependent* scheme of identity and seek to *escape the norm* imposed upon them by the dissociated order (so-called hegemonic masculinity) because they are aware of the value of links and emotions and of the richness of living these actively and consciously. And yet, there are still very few such men, given the costs of accepting the contradictions of independent individuality, and because of how easily they can find women who specialize in the emotional world more than they themselves. In fact, change is even harder than it seems, because when some of these men discover the personal fulfilment that can be gained from knowing and managing their own emotions, their success with women seeking greater levels of equality is such that this change so happily begun may be interrupted and turned into a narcissistic trap, preventing them from taking on the costly struggle inherent in the construction of true *independent individuality*. The percentage of those prepared to go all the way with the difficult (but rich) implications of this type of identity is thus certainly reduced.

Independent individuality is thus an exceptional form of identity among men and, in fact, still scarce among women. At this moment, we find ourselves before an entire set of *transitional* varieties between *independent individuality* and conventional gender identities—*dependent individuality* in men and *relational identity* among women. At no other time in history has there been so much diversity, for no other socioeconomic order has ever been defined by the exercise of specialized functions on the part of both men and women. But to be able to briefly assess the present situation, it is necessary to turn back to the concepts of sex and gender and to the valuable information afforded to us by our dear and closest evolutionary relatives, the bonobos.

References

Giddens, A. (1991). *Modernity and self identity: Self and society in late modern age*. Cambridge: Polity Press.
Valcárcel, A. (2008). *Feminismo en un mundo global*. Madrid: Cátedra.
Walter, N. (2010). *Living dolls: The return of sexism*. London: Virago.

Chapter 10
Sex and Gender All over Again

10.1 On Gender

I have discussed some of the changes undergone by the identities of men and women throughout our history. Chronologically, these can be organized into three phases: (a) a first phase (hunter-gatherer societies) where both sexes' identities were *relational*; (b) a second phase (socially hierarchic premodern societies and most contemporary couples) where men underwent a range of changes toward individuation within *dependent individuality*, while women retained their *relational identity*; and (c) a third phase (which, although only possible in modernity, is still very infrequent) where some women—and, exceptionally, the occasional man—have developed *independent individuality*.

Turning back to the category of *gender*, whose definition has been analyzed in Chap. 2, it is striking how perfectly it overlaps with the identity differences between men and women of the second phase, suggesting an identification of *female identity* with the traits of *relational identity* and an identification of *male identity* with the traits of *dependent individuality*. In this phase, relationships between men and women necessarily imply a power relationship, a partnership, and heterosexual normativity. In turn, the first phase would imply normative heterosexuality as a way of guaranteeing the complementarity of functions, but not necessarily as a power relationship (although possibly one of prestige). Of course, in no way does this imply that couples are the only possible form of relationship between men and women (indeed many ethnological studies have proven that the concept of family can adopt very different meanings). In the third phase—that of *independent individuality*—sexual and affective relationships between individuals do not necessarily require conforming to a norm of compulsory heterosexuality or impose partnerships as permanent couples—although this is indeed one of their possible forms—nor, most importantly, do they entail power relationships.

What Money and Stoller originally identified as *gender* and *gender identity* described a certain situation in the second phase, namely, the identities of 1950s and

1960s middle-class men (*dependent individuality*) and women (*relational identity*) in the United States, at a time when differences in their respective degrees of individuation were at their peak and very widespread (with far more individuated men than, for example, the nineteenth century). This means that Money and Stoller's concept of *gender identity* should not be extrapolated to other historical moments, either within the second phase, or especially, in the other two. Otherwise, we run the risk of considering *feminine* those traits which also characterize, for example, all hunter-gatherers as well as the less individuated men of any historical period, including contemporary culture. Or we risk considering *masculine* the traits of individuality which, as we have seen, operate in women in modernity.

In this respect, I find that the use of the concept of gender entails the risk of *naturalizing* identities which the patriarchal order associates with men and women, which could become a perverse instrument of perpetuation of its logic. Since the concept of *gender* refers to features differentially associated with either men or women, it could be used to argue that *dependent individuality* is the *natural* way of being a man and that *relational identity* is the equivalent for women, as has been commonplace in social discourse. Saying, for example, that a man is very *feminine* because of his distinct sensitiveness or ability to empathize and that a woman is very *masculine* because she exhibits clear ambition for power are not symptoms of change in society but mere restatements of the old idea that power is a representative male attribute, whereas emotion is more suitable for women. This way, a discourse is reinforced where men and women are seen as having "switched sides" when they develop character and identity traits which *naturally* belong only to the other sex. It is because of these risks that I think the concept of gender should be used with caution, as a way of referring to the complementary and unequal identities of men and women of the second phase but without universalizing it for *all* men and women. For the same reason, I am opposed to the use of such concepts as the "third gender" (Herdt 1994), or, in general, to any identification of this category with closed set of traits of any type whatsoever.

Finally, while I agree that the category of gender is inseparable from the patriarchal order, for all the reasons stated above, I am uncertain about its validity in the first phase proposed above and clearly against its use in the third. Imagining a nonpatriarchal society means imagining a society without genders. I can only conceive of two possibilities for nonpatriarchal social formations: (a) one where all people are granted equal importance and are able to consciously develop mechanisms based on reason and emotion, on individuality and on relational identity, i.e., where all people are characterized by *independent individuality*, or (b) one deriving from the former where, once social discourse has recognized that neither reason nor emotion correspond to any essence pertaining to either men or women, different kinds of relationships can prosper between them and be judged equally by all of society. That is, one where women and men are judged equally, whether they dedicate more time to work than to their children, or whether they express their emotions and affections, display ambition for power, or choose to look after their families instead of developing professionally. In both social formations, the identification of women with one social norm and men with another will has been overcome, as well as the impending threat of punishment for breaking such norms. In both cases, gender will have ceased to exist.

If such a point can ever be reached, we still have a long way to go, although a shift has begun to take place. Still, in order to assess the present situation, we need to consider an element which premodern societies disregarded due to the patriarchal order's *naturalization* of a single option and its denial that any other possible options might even exist: the factor of sexual preference.

10.2 On Sexuality

As has been proposed here, the complementarity of male and female functions underpinning social ordering since the earliest stages of *Homo* must have been necessary to raise such dependent and fragile offspring as characterize our genus. Such complementarity might explain why heterosexuality was imposed as the social norm and why, as (*dependent*) masculine individuation progressed, social discourse insisted on considering it a natural law, thus granting continuity to its own underlying fantasy. Under economic, social, and identity imperatives, couples became the *norm*, and the heterosexual stable couple was eventually enshrined as society's *natural* core. But, as descriptions of bonobo life show, the role of human sexuality cannot be restricted to reproduction, as, had this been the case, nature would not have given up the much more efficient—and heterosexual—system of the call of estrus. If nature opted out of estrus, at the expense of its strength, it must have been because the gains were worth the change. And among these gains must have been the increase in communication described above, which boosts group cooperation without requiring any specific sexual preference. Bonobos engage in heterosexual and homosexual relationships alike (we could say they are all bisexual) as their sexuality is their most powerful means of social cementing—not of division or social classification but of group building as such. Far from putting the group's reproduction at risk, this aspect in fact increases cooperation within it. In the case of *Homo*, a similar scenario is quite likely to have been the *natural* starting point, heterosexuality being a norm imposed culturally to see to an offspring who, unlike that of bonobos, is extremely dependent. For this reason, as soon as constraints no longer impose this complementarity (as is the case in modernity), the heterosexual norm also becomes obsolete, and all the possibilities of sexual orientation are opened up.

Anthropological and archaeological evidence allows us to infer that complementarity (whether as monogamous partnership or any other distribution of functions between men and women), and therefore heterosexuality, must have been widespread at the start of historical trajectories. We know, however, that clear examples of affection and sexuality within the same sex have existed throughout history and in a vast majority of cultures. Occasionally, masculine homosexuality has even been sponsored by highly misogynous cultures, whereas female homosexuality—for obvious reasons related to power dynamics—has had to struggle hard to find expression. In any case, time and time again, different types of homosexuality have successfully circumvented the norms and social constructs enshrined as the group's socio-reproductive core. Cultures different from our own have sometimes legitimated homosexuality through what some authors have called a "third gender," or accepted its coexistence with heterosexual relationships (Krige 1974; Kelly 1976; or the classical world), but the norm in the Western world and in the greater part of other cultures has been only one: heterosexuality.

And yet, by carrying out specialized work in modernity, women effectively broke the norm of complementarity, rendering unnecessary the heterosexual norm that granted its compliance. As a result, that other *natural* function of sexuality—communication—returned, and along came free orientation, as can increasingly be appreciated in contemporary sexuality. This fact is as new and as spawned by modernity as women's work specialization, but, by the same token, its mere presence should not be misinterpreted as a resistance to the patriarchal order. Monogamous partnership continues to constitute the prevailing model of organization in modernity, because the patriarchal order continues to guide socialization and the entire economic and social system. Unlike in previous phases, both members of a couple can now have the same level of specialization at their jobs, and even the same sex, without substantially altering the patriarchal logic. I shall explain this.

A quick review of the possible partnerships which surround us reveals that, in addition to the *pure* traditional couples as defined by Money, the contemporary social landscape has become far more varied and flexible. We can find relationships which, at first sight, seem egalitarian, that is, both partners work and appear to enjoy economic autonomy and autonomy of desires, and both partners feature more *mixed* traits (i.e., some relational identity among men and quite some individuality among women). But these appearances all too often hide a greater specialization of men in *dependent individuality*, and in *relational identity* on the part of the women, who are now subjected to a double and extenuating demand that is not pressed on the men. So, although the economic complementarity has disappeared, the model of emotional complementarity remains, allowing us to fool ourselves about the extent to which *advances* have been made toward equality. Or it is possible to find, as is often the case in the United States, heterosexual couples where the woman's specialization in relational identity is less visible (although it continues to exist, translating, for example, into a nonrenounceable need for maternity) as both partners present high levels of *dependent individuality* and, therefore, of dissociated reason-emotion, which allows them to occupy high positions of power. In these cases, emotional deficits are often compensated for by both sides holding a mythical-religious belief (observe the apparent paradox that the United States is the country that most idealizes reason while holding religious beliefs most firmly). Or it is also possible to find traditional roles associated with the opposite sex, also with mixed traits (with men being the more relational part and women being the more individuated), or homosexual couples defined by different levels of that same complementarity in each member of the couple. To all of these we must add people with *independent individuality*, which, I will repeat this again, I consider the only mode which allows us to build truly egalitarian relationships, regardless of each partner's sex. For the reasons specified in Chap. 9, I consider this the only form of identity that allows individuals to live outside of a couple, either alone or in other relationship forms different from traditional couples.

Many years ago, Gayle Rubin (1975: 204) dreamt of "a genderless (though not sexless) society, in which one's sexual anatomy is irrelevant to who one is, what one does, and with whom one makes love." Having developed the present analysis, I have no choice but to partake of her dream. The only nonpatriarchal society I can imagine is one where men and women can choose their sexual orientation freely, where relationships are no longer determined by gender formats associated with each sex but based on the desire to share the emotions and reasons both are capable of generating, valuing, and interpreting. Society cannot possibly overcome patriarchy if women adopt the identity which presently characterizes most men. Only when both men and women can consciously and actively develop the emotional and rational resources which characterize *independent individuality*, or at least when society considers it equally legitimate for either sex to develop either identity *block*, will patriarchy be overcome. At that moment, the concepts of *masculine* and *feminine* will no longer make any sense. Then, society will simply be made up of people who, irrespective of their sex, can be as rational as they are emotional, as intelligent as they are sensitive, as much agents of their own lives as caring of those of the rest. When and if this is the case, their sex will have stopped being the variable which determines, at birth, the position they eventually come to occupy in society.

References

Herdt, G. H. (1994). *Third sex, third gender: Beyond sexual dimorphism in culture and history*. Nueva York: Zone Books.
Kelly, R. C. (1976). Witchcraft and sexual relations. An exploration in the social and semantic implications of the structure of belief. In P. Brown & G. Buchbinder (Eds.), *Man and woman in the New Guinea Highlands* (N° 8, pp. 36–53). Washington: Special Publications of the American Anthropological Association.
Krige, E. J. (1974). Woman-marriage, with special reference to the Lovedu-its significance for the definition of marriage. *Africa Journal of the International African Institute, 44*(1), 11–37.
Rubin, G. (1975). The traffic on women. Notes on the "political economy of sex". In R. R. Reiter (Ed.), *Toward and anthropology of women* (pp. 157–210). New York: Monthly Review Press.

Chapter 11
Conclusion

11.1

Perhaps the past could not possibly have been any different, but, in any case, we cannot change it today. And yet, we do have the duty to think about our future and what we want it to be like as it begins to slip through our fingers. So far, a trend has prevailed in our historical trajectory toward an increased separation between men's specialization in rationalizing the world and women's specialization in securing the bonds of belonging which men's specialization relies on, to allow this to continue.

Since the arrival of modernity, however, women have proven that such a dissociation is not inevitable, that it is possible to master the security mechanisms afforded by reason without denying those related to emotion and group belonging. If one's own emotional needs are acknowledged and met, a far more autonomous and powerful form of identity can be built, one that enables us to make decisions taking into consideration the needs of others while rendering these needs clearer as we learn to recognize our own. The ability to explicitly conjugate emotion and reason and recognize the importance of both is not something that stems from women's bodies or from any particular proclivity toward harmony and sensitivity. It is the mere result of a particular historical process which has forced them (and continues to force them) to recognize the reality of what we are. Interestingly, fundamental aspects of this insight have also been acknowledged by recent neurological and biological studies (Damasio 1994; Fausto-Sterling 2000) as well as by a growing number of male voices (Brooks 2011; Carabí and Armengol 2008; Lomas 2002).

Antonio Damasio (1994), for example, proved how closely and inseparably the neuronal centers interact when guiding actions which had so far been considered to relate to either reason or emotion. His experiments show that it is emotional perception of their surroundings that allows human beings to make effective rational decisions. As stated at the beginning of this book, emotions—and the empathy they allow—enable us to predict the responses to any given action. This allows human beings to assess the convenience of acting in one way or another and to ponder the effectiveness of a certain response against the backdrop of its context. In fact, when victims of accidents suffer from severe neuronal damage are sometimes impaired in such a way that makes them incapable of empathizing or assessing situations on the emotional level, their responses, while possibly correct from the *rational* point of view, actually have disastrous effects on their lives because they fail to meet the adequate needs or expectations. This way, individuals who proceed in a strictly rational fashion can easily lose partners, jobs, and any possibility of social interaction, turning their lives into complete failures. Damasio has proven that when people capable of normal social interaction take decisions which society considers purely *rational*, a complex network of neuronal centers is activated where reason cannot be dissociated from emotion. In fact, "certain aspects of the process of emotion and feeling are indispensable for rationality" (Damasio 1994: xiii). So it is simply untrue that reason can be separated from emotion, even in neurological terms. This fundamental point needs to be acknowledged by any theory of the subject, science, human society, or of power. There is no such thing as reason autonomous from emotion.

11.2

Independent individuality—the identity mode which, since modernity, has characterized growing numbers of women (and exceptionally some men)—recognizes the fundamental interconnected character of reason and emotion. Therefore, defending it as the future identity model for the socialization of men and women does not signify any *female* (or *feminist*) claim. It simply embraces the struggle to accept and recognize the truth about what human beings—both men and women—are made of. This is a truth which has so far been denied by social discourse, due to the failure on the part of the men who have constructed it to recognize the importance of emotions among their own security mechanisms.

As an expression of the identity of those in power, the patriarchal order's dissociated discourse can pervade our social milieu by setting the tone of the policies organizing our social life. Even more importantly, it shapes the subjectivities of those socialized into its dynamics. For this reason, I consider that feminist critique—or whatever we wish to call a type of social critique which acknowledges the complexity of cultural foundations and does not *deny* the value of emotions—is today more necessary than ever because it manifests that the social discourse upheld by our own group does not correspond with the *truth*, that the universe is immeasurably more powerful than human beings, and therefore, that the more we deny, hide, or mask our essential impotence before it, the more we will deny, hide, and muffle our strategies for bonding and belonging as well as those who embody them.

The feminist movement was born when certain intelligent women trained in reason began to *profess* that the Enlightenment should put into practice the alleged *universality* of its principles of justice and equality by including women in the democratic system's claim to guarantee "freedom for the individual in the face of the community" (Cobo 2011: 31). Until then, men had considered these principles to apply only to themselves, as they, certainly in the eighteenth century, were the only ones who embodied *individuality*. In reasoning like this, their discourse effectively justified the exclusion of women from the *universal*,[1] although the argument was shattered, however, when women began to specialize and to educate and individuate themselves. Recognition of the mismatch between the *theory* of discourse and its practical application has caused growing numbers of men to join women in efforts to legislate and apply institutional measures that promote equal rights for all members of society, though equality remains a distant objective. The primal reason for this is that the greater part of society (men and women) continues to embody (to a different extent and sometimes unwittingly) traditional gender identities. Having construed themselves through the mandates of a certain social order, individuals continue to reinforce and reproduce it.

A second reason is that the struggle for equality takes place, in the best of cases, in a purely discursive field, which ultimately signals its basic submission to the very dissociated logic which impedes equality. As I have tried to prove, this discourse has historically been the expression of an identity mode which characterizes men who (in a *fractal* relationship) govern social groups. As they developed power, reason, and individuality, these men concealed the importance of affection and emotions and the need to belong to a community, although they by no means overcame these needs. However much men *denied* them, to the point of becoming utterly unable to recognize these needs, they nonetheless continued to perform them (as was the case with Rathje's garbage archaeology project). Thus, their discourse dealt only with the recognized and visible part, claiming that reason and individuality are the only possible routes to empowerment. This discourse (and the identity that construes it) was definitively consolidated by the Enlightenment, which rose to the category of *truth*, the *denial* that constitutes the patriarchal order's deepest core (and the key to the need for women's subordination). This explains an incompatibility which I consider fundamental between Enlightened thought and feminism, between the subject as defined by the Enlightenment, and a subject who is capable of establishing egalitarian relationships, and, more widely, between the Enlightenment and reclaiming an order which does not require the subordination of women as a precondition for its foundational fantasy.

Enlightened feminism has brought about such transcendental advances in the struggle for equality between the sexes that one cannot but gratefully acknowledge and admire them (Amorós 1997; Valcárcel 1997; Molina Petit 2009; Cobo 2011; among others). These advances are undoubtedly indispensable, for they have exposed the internal incoherencies of enlightened discourse. Enlightened feminism is ultimately responsible for legal and institutional changes, gender monitoring institutions, a less sexist use of language, and a general transformation of discourse in some sectors of society. But, in my opinion, one of the limitations of these

---

[1] Amorós (1987: 113) has referred to how the category of "equals" was used to refer to men, whereas "identical" was applied to women.

advances is that they do not challenge the more profound logic of our social order, its subjection to the dissociation of reason and emotion. The advances made so far have taken place within the bubble of patriarchal discourse, at the level of the fantasy of what we are. But they have failed to recognize our complex and contradictory reality in its entirety and to unmask the incongruences between the *reasoned truth* and the *reality performed* by men and women in our society. Thus, the key upon which this order is founded remains unquestioned. This explains why—seemingly paradoxically—there can be men and women who, while using reason to fight for equality in the public sphere, nonetheless sustain unequal relationships in their private lives. Or, perhaps even more surprisingly, that those who listen to these men and women can be more persuaded by the content of their discourse than by the evidence of their actions. Only by abandoning the discourse which legitimates our present social order (and therefore by abandoning the *truths* which construe it) is it possible to see what discourse *denies*, to shed light (the light of reason) on the part of social behavior which we cannot see although it is right before our eyes or even if we perform it ourselves, as the patriarchal discourse of the Enlightenment has taught us not to recognize it. A true change of the social order will come about only when we recognize that emotions and bonds play as important parts in the construction of security mechanisms in modernity as reason and individuality, and that neither can the individual stand without the community nor can reason exist without emotion. Only then will we truly have questioned the logic which so far has guided modernity, and only then will we understand that a true assessment of the essential contribution made by women to our own historical trajectory requires unmasking the concealment of the *relational* function which the patriarchal order relies on.

I have tried to state clearly that by no means do I agree with postmodern statements of any *essential* differences between men and women—basically rooted in the latter's maternal capacities (Muraro 1991)—nor do I support the nontransferable *particularity* of each subject, which those positions ascribe to a particular combination of circumstances (thus dismantling any strategy of social or political struggle). Reason and individuality constitute fundamental instruments for human empowerment, and my point is simply that this empowerment cannot possibly come about without the links which are crucial to group belonging. In this sense, most feminist positions would seem to have further deepened the dissociation of reason and emotion (obviously unwittingly), reinforcing the patriarchal order's most profound logic. So-called *modern feminism* or *feminism of equality*[2] emphasizes reason, and *postmodern feminism* or *feminism of difference*[3] emphasizes emotion, precluding the defense of a form of politics which contemplates their mutual interdependence. One feels tempted to describe as *post-enlightened* a theory which can incorporate the emotional and unconscious dimension of human behavior while operating with objectively assessable statements (and therefore sustained by reason). Or perhaps it would suffice to include it among the set of positions which comprise the so-called

---

[2] In the English-speaking world this would correspond to *radical feminism* and *socialist feminism*.

[3] In the English-speaking world, *cultural feminism*.

theory of complexity considered at the beginning of this book. Such a theory could be considered *feminist* only insofar as the normative social discourse continues to *deny* that human behavior follows logics which are *complex* (i.e., both conscious and unconscious, simultaneously rational and emotional). As long as such denial continues to dominate, this theory will only represent (in *fractal* relationship) the discourse of those women (and, exceptionally, of some men) with *independent individuality* who aspire to relationships of equality between the sexes.

11.3

I wish to insist that the struggle for *equal rights* for men and women is not an attempt to standardize all individuals' personal identities, but, rather, to put an end to normative stereotypes that either men or women are forced to fit into for the mere fact that their bodies happen to be different. Different subjectivities and abilities will always exist among individuals, and interrelations will always be construed in different ways. In fact, equality will only be a reality when men and women are no longer socially penalized for trespassing the *gender format* prescribed for them (Levinton 2000). Thus, the category of *gender* should be used to describe power relations governing the patriarchal order, but not to design a society of equals.

Society will only change social discourse, which at present *naturalizes* gender, when men (as some already have) become aware of and grant importance to their own emotions. Yet, since the social order continues to be governed by a dissociated logic, the less men embody such dissociation, the less chances they will have to occupy high-ranking positions of power (which we could also express by saying that the more they move away from positions of power, the more *independent* their individuality can be). For the same reason, it is very difficult for women to gain access to high positions of power. They are only allowed to do so at the price of reinforcing patterns of *dependent individuality* (in the exceptional, and in my view, undesirable event that they find couples who represent the complementary relational counterpart), or at exceptionally high prices, which cause most of them to give up trying once they reach the so-called "glass ceiling" (Burín 2003). This term has been proposed to describe the limits of investment in managing one's own professional life for those who need to manage in parallel their emotional networks, families, or friendships. Men effectively delegate the latter in their feminine partners, but women are forced to fulfil both functions for themselves.

Although many women are interested in occupying *intermediate* positions of power—where a direct relationship with the social group is still possible (San José 2003: 165–166)—few are willing to occupy the highest positions of power, which require—regardless of the sexed bodies—playing into a logic and relationship with the world based on the dissociation reason-emotion. As the use of material culture reminds us, the suit and tie also lays down the dress norm for those women who access high positions of power in the Western world: although it might replace pants with skirts, without a tie, and in a wider range of colors, the suit-dress is a suit after all—the power dress of *dependent individuality*. Any other appearance tends to be considered too informal or inappropriate and rarely fails to elicit criticisms and comments which manifest the rules of the game of power.

Some think that the mere access of growing numbers of women to power will eventually alter that logic. For all the reasons stated above, I do not believe that this—certainly necessary—process will be sufficient in and of itself. Women should be aware that the *independent individuality* most of them embody is the identity mode of a future, more egalitarian, and fairer society, unlike the *dependent individuality* which defines most of their partners. Also, the hypothesis that allowing women access to institutions of power will automatically cause them to be represented at parity with men seems guided by the same *denial* which is so typical of the present dissociated order: if men in power continue embodying *dependent individuality*, they will continue to need women who prioritize their *relational identity*—although they may work at the same time—and the system will continue to foster this through all mechanisms available. Unless men's *rational* anti-domination discourse (whether sexual, political, social, or personal) is coupled with egalitarian relationships in their own personal lives, their discourses and their *reasons* cannot possibly be effective, because they will continue to be trapped in the contradiction of preventing that which they nonetheless *believe to be fighting for*. Only when one does not participate in power relationships in day-to-day life can one truly struggle for a different destiny for the whole group. As Kate Millet (1970) said so many years ago, the personal is always political (another way of referring to its *fractal* relationship). So, stating that it would suffice to open up institutional doors for women, who, guided by their *free* will, shall proceed to even up the figures, is just another way of denying that the (traditional) male exercise of power is based on and requires female subordination. For, while they might publicly espouse equality, men will continue to demand women's subordination in their private lives. Not acknowledging this is another way of refusing to understand that human identity does not depend on freely exercised volitional capacities but on the subjective effectiveness of ideas long transmitted to us about who we are in the socialization process.

This affects both men and women, for, as I have insisted, men's subjectivity, too, is the result of socialization, and, unfortunately, men continue to be trained in unawareness and lack of attention toward emotions. Although some men begin to value and become conscious of emotions, it should not be forgotten that the patriarchal order places them in a position of power and privilege, making it much harder for them to question its underlying logic fully and in depth. For this reason, men, with exceptions, cannot be expected to lead the struggle for this transformation. Of course, they would gain true autonomy and power, but on a very different basis from that which the system's legitimizing discourse is prepared to recognize. It therefore seems far more likely that only when the great majority of men have difficulty finding women who clearly prioritize their *relational* side will they be forced to look after their own emotional world and transform the political logic.

For the same reasons, a transformation of the social order requires first a transformation in the subjectivity of the majority of women, a situation which appears very distant. As has been shown, just as many men, whose discourse is explicitly pro-equality, continue to sustain profoundly unequal relationships with their partners, just so there are women who, while defending discourses in favor of equality, nonetheless continue to mobilize subjectivities modeled by identification with a subordinate position (and demand from their male partners what their discourse claims to combat). Actual lack of self-esteem and of trust in their own capacities or difficulties in defining desires *for oneself* are still visible symptoms of many women who, on the surface, would seem highly individuated. The construction of a truly *independent individuality* constitutes a slow and very gradual process, as it does not depend on these women's *wills* but on the transformation of models reinforced in socialization through the constant effort of those who already embody this identity mode.

At this point, we are faced with a subtle but profound problem, which proves the perverse and effective nature of our social order's *regime of truth*. We have stated that the struggle for equality must defend both the individualized *set* of reason and the relational one of emotion as essential for survival. Since women have historically been characterized by only developing the latter, many of today's women dedicate their efforts to emphasizing the importance of the former as a way of obtaining autonomy and independence (thereby following Enlightened convictions). This would not be a problem were it not for the fact that, in many cases, they reject or at least forget the importance of relational identity, replicating and reinforcing the very logic they intend to combat. If only those features associated with individuality (creativity, use of reason, sense of risk) are granted importance, and if all our efforts are directed at highlighting women scientists, intellectuals, artists, travelers, or explorers, we run the risk of perversely reinforcing patriarchal discourse, through an unwitting contribution to the consolidation of its cornerstone. This is a complex and difficult problem, as power establishes a *filter* to select for society's highest positions those who devote all their time and energy to rational ways of engaging with the world and to develop policies (academic, economic, social) based on the dissociation of reason and emotion. Therefore, if those women who struggle for equality emphasize only the individuated part of identity, that is, only the mechanisms of reason, it might happen that an ever-growing number of women *will* be recognized by the patriarchal order…but only at the price of having adapted to its logic!

11.4

It could be argued that men and women *already* tend to grant importance to their emotional and family world. In fact, paradoxically, the very men who devote most time, energy, and dedication to intellectual or specialized work or to sustaining a position of power (therefore not to their children or families) are those who most explicitly declare these to be the most important things in their lives. Similarly, many individuated women could not possibly develop their professional work without the support they gain (in terms of identity) from having children or a partner. We all grant importance to our emotions and our private personal support network, but the problem is that this *recognition is limited to the private realm and does not permeate social discourse*, because we all (both men and women) still consider that, as dictated by patriarchal discourse, emotion pertains to the private realm and reason to the public arena. Since the public realm continues to be a masculine domain, the upbringing of young boys still involves the repression of emotions (and therefore, of empathy, of care for the other, and of sensitivity), while girls continue to be raised to specialize in emotions, resituating the sexes back to a dichotomy of domination and subordination and reinforcing an increasingly dissociated discourse of truth-power. By the *fractal* logic described at the beginning of this book, the professional and public worlds still claim to be guided exclusively by objective and rational criteria, causing *denial* to be projected onto the very construction of social science, which, in a seemingly endless loop, legitimates and reproduces this discourse.

As a result, the criteria of *excellence* espoused by positive sciences, which specialize in the study of nonhuman phenomena, are being transferred to disciplines that deal with human phenomena, what causes critique, profound reflection, and the questioning of paradigms and social discourse to lose ground.[4] Physicians and mathematicians are increasingly requested to explain and design economic trends, the future that we have to prepare ourselves for, as human beings are less and less recognized in their humanity, in their complex particularities, and increasingly detached from their own depth and richness, from what they cannot control, from what they fear, their own insufficiencies, and their impotence…detached from the entire set of transcendental mechanisms of their emotional worlds.

Google identifies the brain with an information processor and intelligence with efficient data processing, struggling to create ever-faster search engines to—in their opinion—improve the intelligence of users (Carr 2010: 152, 167, 172–173). Increasingly, social discourse insists on comparing human beings, not just with nonhuman dynamics, as *positive science* used to (and continues to do), but also with machines, definitively *denying* the emotional dimension and awareness of its complexity.

Science and its institutions generate our society's *truth*, one which insists more and more on emotional *denial*. The humanities and social sciences are losing their social *value* and are invariably subjected to the same productive demands expected of technical laboratories, decidedly favoring the most technical and least complex, the most quantitative and mechanistic positions. Dissociation is increasing to the extent that, when it comes to social sciences and the humanities, the pursuit of knowledge and of academic power are goals which nowadays appear to only coincide exceptionally, and represent increasingly divergent and mutually exclusive paths. Each one has its own rules, its rhythms, and, in the case of non-English-speaking countries, its own languages to communicate knowledge.

---

[4] Interestingly, the Excellence Baccalaureate implemented by the Madrid Regional Government (*Comunidad Autónoma de Madrid*) in the academic year 2011–2012 to incorporate and promote students with the best academic records in the region will have four Sciences groups and one Humanities group, as demanded by the students themselves.

The English language—in Sennett's words (1998) the *lingua franca* of new capitalism and undoubtedly that of Hardt and Negri's (2000) *Empire*, expression of the most (dependently) individuated identities in the world, has embarked on global dominance as the single structure through which to conceive reality. Classes in English are becoming the norm at Spanish universities, a change which might be useful and convenient in more technical fields but a complete hindrance in those which require critical thought, because thinking in a foreign language limits thought to the more rational aspects of a problem, leaving out its emotional connotations. The use of English could end up reinforcing the effects once held by prestige Latin (or rabbinic Hebrew, classic Arabic, Sanskrit, and classic Chinese in other cultures), such as favoring the individuation and power of certain elites (who could afford training in them and which in the case of classical languages were exclusively masculine), by, among other mechanisms, associating knowledge with "a vehicle away from the emotionally charged-up depths of (the) mother tongue" (Ong 1982: 114). The widespread use of English would increase the emotional distance between the knowing agent and the known object. In this way, interpretations of things human are fostered which obliterate the emotional dimension, both of those who construe the accounts and of their protagonists.

11.5

The drift of changes currently facing the Western world makes it more necessary than ever to keep a critical stance before the order and values governing the system. Criticisms are voiced in this direction in the quarters of sociology and economics but, although the present situation is the sheer expression of the patriarchal order's hypertrophy, those authors only exceptionally connect both aspects (Torres López 2010; Gálvez and Torres López 2010, for example).

In fact, the Internet is fostering an entire set of changes which we must be aware of if we are to design new strategies in the struggle for equality. Writing once constituted an "intellectual technology"[5] which, as a rationalization tool, contributed to an increase in dissociation, although at the same time it enabled women to become aware of and combative about their own rights. Similarly, although the Internet may help take a further step in individual levels of dissociation, it carries a great potential for communication and relationships. As many contemporary social movements have proven, this potential could be used to transform society in ways which would otherwise appear inconceivable.

As noted above, writing was an *intellectual technology* invented by men at the highest levels of individuation attainable in an oral society. It was used unwittingly and in an unplanned way to respond to a demand which would allow society to continue the logic of changes which already characterized it. The changes brought about by the Internet represent a quantitative leap comparable to the transition from

---

[5] See note 2 of Chap. 5.

oral society to a society with writing. We are now facing a new *intellectual technology* which, far from constituting a merely technical tool, has as much capacity to transform identities—and consequently social dynamics—as literacy had with respect to orality. As in that remote step in our historical trajectory, the Internet has been imagined by men with *dependent individuality* at a time when the prevailing tools to represent the world (derived back then from orality, and nowadays from writing) appear to have exhausted the possibilities of increasing abstraction and the subsequent degree of rationalization and individuation brought on by increased dynamics of socioeconomic complexity.

The Internet grants access to a different level of reality inaccessible to writing. While in orality human beings establish direct relationships with *things*, and in writing they do so with *representations of things*, on the Internet, relations are established with *representations of the appearance of things*. This opens up possibilities for a much wider world, but, at the same time, could possibly detach human beings even further from emotional and sensitive connection with themselves and their surroundings. The Internet not only comprises the present and the lived past as real phenomena (as orality does), or the present and the non-lived past (as writing does), but also establishes a way of operating with the constructed world through a constant feedback between present and future. The Internet operates in the sheer realm of virtuality, predicting and calculating the value of future products to be developed by the use of present technologies and anticipating the direction of trends. Its ultimate aim is to act ahead of the rest, to come first, to lead. Its power is based on present-future loops, which basically require control over information. Whichever player has more information will wield more power, as they develop a greater capacity to manipulate, direct, transform, encourage, block, and place themselves at an advantage. This way, power loses its connection with land ownership (as in feudalism) or capital (as in modern capitalism). Instead, it becomes associated with information access and control. Žižek (2004: 192–195) coined the term *netocracy* for the new elite brought about by the Internet, which is capable of controlling economic, social, and, of course, personal dynamics through its control over network information. Power increasingly consists in possessing the immaterial, in change and acceleration, in extreme rationalization, in *total emotional detachment*.

Mercantilist capitalism has given way to brutally speculative and financial capitalism, embodied by men making decisions at a level so abstract and detached from their (disastrous) effects, that they appear to behave like machines and not people (Stiglitz 2002; Torres López 2010). The feeling of power generated by the Internet requires, in turn, an accelerated change which acquires a qualitative (and not just quantitative) consistency different from all our previous history (as was the case with the transition from orality to writing). Control over information requires constant updating, an uninterrupted connection with the outer world, hyperactive action. More than ever, living is made of appearance and change, although we may not be able to specify either the direction of the latter or the reasons which make it so mandatory, and despite the scant attention paid to the consequences of these changes on the people they affect or in those who promote them. To wield power, one must herald change and live in it. The acceleration is such that it prevents connection, attachment to situations which we are about to abandon at the very moment of initiating them, precluding the stability of affection and the cementing of conscious bonds. Sennett (1998: 61–62) saw in this "lack of attachment" precisely one of the keys to the success of those (overwhelmingly men) who lead the World Economic Forum annually held in Davos (Switzerland) and, specifically, of those who have led and continue to lead change on the Internet.

And yet, as we have seen throughout these pages, human beings need to retain their sense of belonging and bonds in order to feel safe. So if they continue to lose sight of the importance of bonds and their own capacity to build these, there will be no other solution but to boost the unconscious mechanisms which grant them. This way, if this trend continues, and unless it is met with attempts to neutralize it, we can only expect an increase in the two mechanisms which throughout history have operated to compensate *dependent individuality*: gender inequality and unconscious strategies of ascription to groups of peers.

A visibly notorious increase in prostitution and pornography (Walter 2010; Cobo 2011: 91) is already bringing to the surface greater levels of gender inequality. The data show that these are being consumed by younger men than ever before and, as noted by Szil, in search, not of sex (which they can easily get through their everyday relationships), but of power.[6] Prostitution presently represents the third highest source of profits in the capitalist and globalized world, closely following the arms and drug industries (Cobo 2005: 81). Notably, all three are related to that profound process of emotional detachment and dehumanization which increasingly defines the trajectory of the Western world. But there is no need to go so far to notice that the objectification and reification of women are on the rise: breast implants are sought by intelligent and highly attractive women, as well as by younger and younger girls, who expect of themselves to *be liked* more than ever, while suffering more eating disorders than ever. Young women take part in beauty contests and *hot* parties in the naive conviction that they are guided by a newly acquired *freedom* of women's desire (Walter 2010). Maternity and the ability to excite masculine desire appear to be on the rise in the stock market of today's expectations of women, which hardly comes as a surprise given the unstoppable ascent of the *dependent individuality* model as the identity norm among men with power.

With respect to the second type of strategies—male ascription to groups of peers—the highly addictive component often highlighted about new technologies (mobile phones and the Internet) stems precisely from their power to create a sense of belonging, bonds, and connection (Carr 2010). Social or academic networks, net gaming, blogs, etc., are substituting (or being added to) football teams, nationalist identities, political parties, or pressure groups, among the unconscious strategies available to generate a feeling of belonging to groups of peers. Showing that we have *friends* on social networks, that we are "consumed" by others who follow our pages, answer our text messages and e-mails, or react to our *tweets*, is not so much proof of our success as validation that we belong to a human group. Faced with the growing enormity of the task of providing our own lives with meaning, we are

---

[6] Psychotherapist Péter Szil interviewed by Chavarría (2008).

increasingly filled with anxiety to build networks of belonging (Bolstanki and Chiapello 2005: 364). Frustratingly, however, when we finally succeed in building these networks, we find that they bring into play a less and less significant part of ourselves (basically, our appearance) and this generates a constant anxiety to expand networks further, to permanently keep in touch, to guarantee an authenticity which we seem to have lost, and which we no longer know when or where to look for.

In the same way as learning to write used to individuate a person in past times, someone who acquires digital training today is further individuated by their training, at the increased risk of dissociation. However, as I have stated, the tool itself always contains the possibility of combatting that very risk. In fact, the Internet's very potential for network and community building can allow us to escape the isolation and the extreme individuation it can cause in itself, if we do not lose sight of the emotional dynamics it brings into play. This can only be attained through critical reflection and by insistently reclaiming the necessary awareness about our own emotional world.

11.6

The patriarchal order's failure to understand the potential benefits of valuing emotions socially—and promoting them in education—is causing it to fight its present battles even more bitterly on every front. The most dangerous of these could perhaps be the unwitting, unplanned, and unconscious decisions, as this is often the level at which the construction of the regime of *truth* lies, indissociably linked to power strategies. It is striking, for example, to see the publicity given to studies which *naturalize* genetic, hormonal, and cerebral differences between the sexes, as opposed to the scarce visibility granted to research which questions or refutes these differences, or even to research which simply insist that genes are activated—and brain cell synapses modeled—*through experience* and that the biological and the cultural operate in constant codetermination, in the complex patterns of interactions described at the beginning of this book. Sociobiology also inundates explanations of human behavior for the similar reason that the paradigms prevailing in science do not admit to disorder, chaos, or complexity in the processes they study, whether natural or human. Simplified and unreal models are constructed to reassure us that the world around us operates like a machine which can be disassembled and analyzed in different separate components. All of this is proposed to generate the fantasy that we can control that which we cannot, for the simple reason that the universe we inhabit is sheer interaction and complexity, and that it contains us as one of its minuscule particles.

To the vast majority of those in positions of power in the present social order, the possibility of attributing value to emotions in the discourse of truth is inconceivable. In fact, this would entail such a profound transformation of the bases underpinning our system that it would mean a transformation of the very rhythms and priorities which define it. To begin with, it would slow down the acceleration which we are increasingly subjected to. Living our lives with an awareness of the value of emotions means understanding that there is a part of security which comes from stability, from recurrence and permanence, and that without these, *change* can cause great distress (Sennett 1998). Such awareness would not mean that the group's security mechanisms suddenly disappear. On the contrary, recognition of the true dynamics governing human beings would promote policies far more realistic and less destructive, both for the group itself and for its relationships with (human and nonhuman) others, which would strengthen the basis for trust in survival on real terms and not on mere appearances of power. This is crucial not only to achieve equality between men and women, but also for otherwise the world will be guided by policies designed for machines, which in fact determine the fates of real people, enforced by politicians whose decision-making abilities will be severely and uncontrolledly hampered by their unacknowledged fears, insecurities, narcissisms, and fragilities.

If the direction and uncontrolled pace being imposed upon social change by this dissociated (patriarchal) order are not reversed, we run the risk of designing policies which are increasingly cut off from human realities, from the true emotional needs of citizens and from the sustainability of the planet and of social peace. Never before has a (feminist) critique of the dissociation underlying the power that governs us been so necessary. And, for this very reason, such a critique is likely to be resisted by (patriarchal) social discourse like never before.

References

Amorós, C. (1987). Espacio de los iguales, espacio de las idénticas. Notas Sobre Poder y Principio de Individuación. *Arbor, 128,* 503–504.
Amorós, C. (1997). *Tiempo de feminismo. Sobre feminismo, proyecto ilustrado y postmodernidad.* Madrid: Cátedra.
Bolstanki, L., & Chiapello, E. (2005). *The new spirit of capitalism.* Nueva York: Verso.
Brooks, D. (2011). *The social animal. Hidden sources of love, character and achievement.* Nueva York: Random House.
Burín, M. (2003). El deseo de poder en la construcción de la subjetividad femenina. El 'techo de cristal' en la carrera laboral de las mujeres. In A. Hernando (Coord.), *¿Desean las mujeres el poder? Cinco reflexiones en torno a un deseo conflictivo* (pp. 33–70). Madrid: Minerva.
Carabí, Á., & Armengol, J. M. (Eds.). (2008). *La masculinidad a debate.* Barcelona: Icaria.
Carr, N. (2010). *The shallows: What the Internet is doing to our brains.* New York: W.W. Norton.
Chavarría, M. (2008, April 12). Una mujer sumisa para acabar bien la noche. *La Vanguardia,* p. 34.
Cobo, R. (2005). El género en las Ciencias Sociales. *Cuadernos de Trabajo Social, 18,* 249–258.
Cobo, R. (2011). Hacia una nueva política sexual. In *Las mujeres ante la reacción patriarcal.* Catarata: Madrid.
Damasio, A. (1994). *Descartes' error.* New York: G.P. Putnam.
Fausto-Sterling, A. (2000). *Sexing the body: Gender politics and the construction of sexuality.* New York: Basic Books.
Gálvez, L., & López, J. T. (2010). Desiguales. In *Mujeres y hombres frente a la crisis económica.* Barcelona: Icaria.
Hardt, M., & Negri, A. (2000). *Empire.* Cambridge, MA: Harvard University Press.

Levinton, N. (2000). Normas e ideales del formato de género. In A. Hernando (Coord.), *La construcción de la subjetividad femenina* (pp. 53–99). Madrid: Instituto de Investigaciones Feministas.

Lomas, C. (Ed.). (2002). *¿Todos los hombres son iguales? Identidad masculina y cambios sociales*. Barcelona: Paidós.

Millet, K. (1970). *Sexual politics*. New York: Doubleday.

Molina Petit, C. (2009). *Dialéctica feminista de la ilustración*. Barcelona: Anthropos.

Muraro, L. (1991). *L'ordine simbolico della madre*. Roma: Editori Riuniti.

Ong, W. (1982). *Orality and literacy. The technologizing of the word*. Londres: Routledge.

San José, B. (2003). De la impotencia al 'empoderamiento'. In A. Hernando (Coord.), *¿Desean las mujeres el poder? Cinco reflexiones en torno a un deseo conflictivo* (pp. 137–169). Madrid: Minerva Ediciones.

Sennett, R. (1998). *The corrosion of character: The personal consequences of work in the new capitalism*. New York: Norton.

Stiglitz, J. E. (2002). *Globalization and its discontents*. New York: WW. Norton.

Torres López, J. (2010). *La crisis de las hipotecas basura. ¿Por qué se cayó todo y no se ha hundido nada?* Madrid: Sequitur.

Valcárcel, A. (1997). *La política de las mujeres*. Madrid: Cátedra.

Walter, N. (2010). *Living dolls: The return of sexism*. London: Virago.

Žižek, S. (2004). *Organs without bodies: Deleuze and consequences*. London: Routledge.

Index

A
Australopithecus, 25, 28, 30, 34
Awá, 48–50

B
Bell Beaker culture, 101
Bell Beaker pottery, 100
Bonobos, 32–36, 53
Bronze Age "toilet articles", 101

C
Casual promiscuity, 26
Civilization and Its Discontents, 5
Civilizing process, 58
Communication, 36

D
Denial of the emotional dimension, 7
Dependent individuality, 82, 85, 86, 97, 129, 130, 135
   description, 108
   diagram of, 108
   emotional dynamics, 109
   hegemonic masculinity, 109
   hunter-gatherers, 110
   narcissism, 109
   patriarchal science, 110
   reason and change mechanisms, 108
   type of power, 109
   unacknowledged and denied strategies, 107
Dialectic of Enlightenment, 7
Dissociated reason-emotion order, 10, 11
Domination of women, 10

E
Eastern Mediterranean merchant incursions, 101
Egalitarian hunter-gatherer society, 6
Egalitarian Societies, 23
   Awá, 50
   ethnological literature, 51
   FUNAI, 48, 49
   gender relations, 52
   marriages, 49
   men and women activities, 50, 51
   power relations, 53
   socioeconomic complexity, 46
   subjectivities and symbolic aspects, 48
Emotional bonds, 14
Emotional dynamics, 109
Emotions, 7, 131
Empathy, 125
Enlightened feminism, 127
Enlightenment, 7–9, 127, 128

F
Fantasy of individuality, 8
Female gender identity, 43, 83
Feminine qualities, 9
Feminism, defined, 110
Feminist, 129
Feminist movement, 126
Filter, 131
Fractal relationship, 5

G
Gender. *See* also Egalitarian Societies
   definition, 19
   male and female identity, 20

Gender (cont.)
    masculinity and femininity, 20, 21
    power relationship, 20, 21, 23
    women characteristics, 22
Gender and individuation process, 120
Gender and Internet, 135
Gender and neoliberal social order, 128
Gender and sex
    anthropological and archaeological evidence, 121
    feminine and masculine traits, 120
    independent individuality, 119
    mixed traits, 122
    monogamous partnership, 122
    nonpatriarchal social formations, 120
    phases, 119
    relational identity, 119
    "switched sides", 120
    "third gender", 122
Gender identities, 20, 36
Genus Homo sexuality, 121
Groups of chiefs, 100

H
Hegemonic masculinity, 99, 109
Hermaphrodites, 19, 20
Historical Western men construction of identity, 70–76
Homo origin
    chimpanzee, 25, 26
    communication, 36
    gorillas, 25
    mobility, 37
    sexuality, 37
    symbols usage, 36
Homo sapiens, origin, 13
Humanity and Primate Behavior Patterns
    Australopithecus, 27, 28, 30, 34
    Bonobos, 31, 32
    chimpanzee, 29, 31, 33
    growth of intelligence, 27
    Homo, 28
    Homo stage, 27
    language, 33
    Neoteny B, 29, 30
    Papio baboons, 27
    sexual dimorphism, 30
    sexuality, 33
Hunter-gatherer societies, 52

I
Identity and socioeconomic complexity, 73
Identity construction's Mechanisms, 12, 13

Identity on conscious level, 70, 72
Identity transformations, 57
Independent individuality, 126, 129–131
    constant demands, 112
    constant, inevitable and everyday contradiction, 113
    contradictory traits, 114
    diagram of, 112
    emotional sustentation, 110
    friendship, defined, 115
    maladjustment, 116
    maximal percentage of, 112
    modernity, 112
    occupied specialized positions, 110
    personal fulfilment, 117
    profound friendships, 115
    relational set, 114
    sexualization and objectification, 115
    social discourse, 115
    socialization model, 111
    transitional varieties, 117
    unacceptable social fault, 115
Individuality
    emotional dynamics, 64
    intellectual technology, 60
    labor specialization, 57
    language, 61
    power, 59
    reflexivity, 63
    self-confidence, 57
    self-esteem and security, 63
    social discourse, 59, 66
    social interaction, 58
    socioeconomic complexity, 58, 60
    structural traits, 63, 64
    success and power, 65
    writing, 61, 62
Individuality as denial of bond emotions, 64–66
Individuation, 15, 52
Individuation process, 71, 72, 76
Intellectual technologies, 60, 133
Internet, 134

L
Lack of attachment, 135
Legitimating discourse, 14

M
Male (unconscious) relational identity
    ascriptive/relational identities, 98
    Bell Beaker grave goods, 101
    bidirectional interaction, 98

dependent individuality, 97, 103
economic and political, 102
exogamous relations, 97
groups of chiefs, 100
hegemonic masculinity, 99
masculine motifs, 101
mythical belief, 104
prestige-goods economies, 99
regional dress, 97
religious and ceremonial symbols, 104
secondary product revolution, 99
socioeconomic trends, 101
unconscious relational identities, 99
V-shaped perforation, 100
Male and female degrees of individuation, 23
Male peer groups, 101
Material culture, 5
Medieval "feminine religious movement", 90
Men's and women's specialization, 125
Money, 20
Myth
  defined, 44
  discourse of origins, 44
  insecurity and impotence, 46
  socioeconomically complex, 46
  space, 45

N
Neoteny B, 28–30
Netocracy, 134
Normative heterosexuality, 82, 85

O
Oligarchic-hierarchic, 28
Orality *vs*. Literacy, 60–62

P
Pan paniscus and Homo sapiens
  communication and cohesion tool, 35
  gender norm, 35
  horticulturalist groups, 35
  hunting activities, 34
  mobility, 35
Patriarchal discourse, 69, 128
Patriarchal order, 10, 12, 136
Patriarchy
  dichotomies, 3
  material culture, 4, 5
  power relationship, 2
  regime of truth, 2, 3

Personal relationships, 4
Positive science, 132
Positivism, 3
Positivist model, 6
Power identity, 126
Power relations, 53
Power relationship, 20
Power
  defined, 57
  inequality, 9
Prestige-goods economies, 99
Principles of Geology, 59
Problem of inequality, 11
Prostitution and pornography, 135
Psychosexual identity, 20

Q
Queer Theory, 19

R
Reason-emotion dissociation, 79, 82, 84–87, 92
Reason-emotion relationship, 125, 126, 128, 129
Reflexivity, 63
Regime of truth, 131
Relational identity, 130
  appearance, 43
  Canaco, 42
  egalitarian societies, 41
  female gender identity, 43
  self-perception, 42
  structural features, 47

S
Secondary product revolution, 80, 87, 99
Self-identity construction
  abstract and rational academic discipline, 72
  community (of believers), 72
  contemporary research, 70
  contemporary society, 76
  control and expertise, 73
  hunter-gatherers, 73
  identity traits, 75
  individuation process, 71
  intellectual developments, 71
  irrigation systems, fertilizer dung/ploughs, 71
  men's individuation process, 76
  oppression/exploitation levels, 75
  plural identities, 75

Self-identity construction (*cont.*)
  power/control/rational knowledge, 74
  relational and individual traits, 70
  relational/individuated identity, 74
  separate blocks/sets of traits, 70
  socioeconomic complexity, 73
  unequal gender relationships and ascribed membership to peer groups, 76
Social order transformation, 130
Society
  characterized, 6
  transformations, 6
Sociobiology, 136

T
Theory of complexity, 8, 129
Tucson Garbage Project, 2

U
Universality, 126

V
Value of emotions, 137
V-shaped perforation, 100

W
Western modern female identity, 110, 111, 115
Women and gender identity
  decision-making processes, 79
  dependent individuality, 82, 85, 86
  family networks, 84
  female gender identity, 83
  mobility, 87–93
  necropolises in Balkans, 80
  normative gender models, 85
  normative heterosexuality, 85
  personal potency, 81
  power and individuated identities, 80
  prehistory manuals, 79
  relational/gender identity, 87
  unplanned and undirected process, 81

GPSR Compliance

The European Union's (EU) General Product Safety Regulation (GPSR) is a set of rules that requires consumer products to be safe and our obligations to ensure this.

If you have any concerns about our products, you can contact us on

ProductSafety@springernature.com

In case Publisher is established outside the EU, the EU authorized representative is:

Springer Nature Customer Service Center GmbH
Europaplatz 3
69115 Heidelberg, Germany

www.ingramcontent.com/pod-product-compliance
Lightning Source LLC
LaVergne TN
LVHW011001250326
834688LV00003B/58